# Grief Diaries

## Hit by Impaired Driver

True stories about being
hit by a drunk, drugged,
distracted or impaired driver

LYNDA CHELDELIN FELL
with
MICHAEL GERSHE
JULIE DOWNS

FOREWORD BY MICHAEL GERSHE
Founder, The Magic of Life

A portion of proceeds from the sale of this book is
donated to The Magic of Life, a nonprofit working
to provide impaired driving education with heart,
soul and humor.   www.themagicoflife.org

AlyBlue
MEDIA

Grief Diaries
Hit by Impaired Driver– 1st ed.
True stories about being hit by a drunk, drugged, distracted, or impaired driver.
Lynda Cheldelin Fell/Julie Downs/Michael Gershe
Grief Diaries www.GriefDiaries.com

Cover Design by AlyBlue Media, LLC
Interior Design by AlyBlue Media LLC
Published by AlyBlue Media, LLC

ISBN: 978-1-944328-49-8
Library of Congress Control Number: 2017901995
AlyBlue Media, LLC
Ferndale, WA 98248
www.AlyBlueMedia.com

PRINTED IN THE UNITED STATES OF AMERICA

AlyBlue
MEDIA

GRIEF DIARIES

# TESTIMONIALS

"CRITICALLY IMPORTANT . . . I want to say to Lynda that what you are doing is so critically important." –DR. BERNICE A. KING, Daughter of Dr. Martin Luther King

"INSPIRATIONAL . . . Grief Diaries is the result of heartfelt testimonials from a dedicated and loving group of people. By sharing their stories, the reader will find inspiration and a renewed sense of comfort as they move through their own journey." -CANDACE LIGHTNER, Founder of MADD

"DEEPLY INTIMATE . . . Grief Diaries is a deeply intimate, authentic collection of narratives that speak to the powerful, often ambiguous, and wide spectrum of emotions that arise from loss. I so appreciate the vulnerability and truth embedded in these stories, which honor and bear witness to the many forms of bereavement that arise in the aftermath of death." -DR. ERICA GOLDBLATT HYATT, Chair of Psychology, Bryn Athyn College

"BRAVE . . . The brave individuals who share their truth in this book do it for the benefit of all." CAROLYN COSTIN, Founder, Monte Nido Treatment Centers

"VITAL . . . Grief Diaries: Surviving Loss of a Pregnancy gives voice to the thousands of women who face this painful journey every day. Often alone in their time of need, these stories will play a vital role in surrounding each reader with warmth and comfort as they seek understanding and healing in the aftermath of their own loss." -JENNIFER CLARKE, obstetrical R.N., Perinatal Bereavement Committee at AMITA Health Adventist Medical Center

"HOPE AND HEALING . . . You are a pioneer in this field and you are breaking the trail for others to find hope and healing." -KRISTI SMITH, Bestselling Author & International Speaker

"A FORCE . . .The writers of this project, the Grief Diaries anthology series, are a force to be reckoned with. I'm betting we will be agents of great change." -MARY LEE ROBINSON, Author and Founder of Set an Extra Plate initiative

"MOVING . . . In Grief Diaries, the stories are not only moving but often provide a rich background for any mourner to find a gem of insight that can be used in coping with loss. Reread each story with pen in hand and you will find many that are just right for you." -DR. LOUIS LAGRAND, Author of Healing Grief, Finding Peace

"HEALING . . . Grief Diaries gives voice to a grief so private, most women bear it alone. These diaries can heal hearts and begin to build community and acceptance to speak the unspeakable. Share this book with your sisters, mothers, grandmothers and friends who have faced grief. Pour a cup of tea together and know that you are no longer alone." -DIANNA VAGIANOS ARMENTROUT, Poetry Therapist & Author of Walking the Labyrinth of My Heart: A Journey of Pregnancy, Grief and Infant Death

"INCREDIBLE . . .Thank you so much for doing this project, it's absolutely incredible!"-JULIE MJELVE, Founder, Grieving Together

"STUNNING . . . Grief Diaries treats the reader to a rare combination of candor and fragility through the eyes of the bereaved. Delving into the deepest recesses of the heartbroken, the reader easily identifies with the diverse collection of stories and richly colored threads of profound love that create a stunning read full of comfort and hope." -DR. GLORIA HORSLEY, President, Open to Hope Foundation

"WONDERFUL . . .Grief Diaries is a wonderful computation of stories written by the best of experts, the bereaved themselves. Thank you for building awareness about a topic so near and dear to my heart." -DR. HEIDI HORSLEY, Adjunct Professor, School of Social Work, Columbia University, Author, Co-Founder of Open to Hope Organization

"GLOBAL . . .One of The Five Facets of Healing mantras is together we can heal a world of hurt. This anthology series is testimony to the power we have as global neighbors to do just that." -ANNAH ELIZABETH, Founder of The Five Facets of Healing

# DEDICATION

This book is dedicated to every victim of drunk, drugged, distracted, or impaired driving.

# CONTENTS

BY MICHAEL GERSHE

# FOREWORD

When I was asked to write this foreword, I was humbled and honored—and then reality set in. Could I write something that represents not just me but all the writers in this book? I've been a victim and survivor of a drunk driving crash that occurred forty-six years ago. It killed my mother and nearly killed me when I was barely eight weeks old. For the last twenty years, I've dedicated my life to educating others about the dangers of it. When I present my program "The Magic of Life," I share my story for three main reasons: to speak for my mother and my family, to speak for others who are impacted by drunk driving but don't have the opportunity to share their story, and to encourage readers to take the keys from an impaired driver before they hurt themselves or someone else. *Grief Diaries: Hit by Impaired Driver* is full of powerful, emotional stories from people who have been impacted by an impaired driver. In America, two in three people will be involved in a drunk driving crash during their lifetime. Drunk driving doesn't discriminate. It impacts all of us, no matter our color, religion, or economic background.

The people sharing their stories in this book are finding their voice, perhaps for the first time, because they want you to know how impaired driving affected them. Millions are injured every year, and thousands die every year from drunk and drugged driving. It's become socially acceptable to drive under the influence—just look at the many celebrities and professional athletes who've been arrested for drunk driving. Many are considered heroes for what they do on the big screen, in the field, pool, or on the court. The majority of society will say, "Oh well, they took responsibility for their actions," after they release a statement to the press. Sure, *after* they've been caught. What about all the other times they put innocent lives at risk, including their own? Did you know that a first-time DUI offender drives drunk at least eighty to ninety times before being caught? If that doesn't shock you, I don't know what will.

With *Grief Diaries: Hit by Impaired Driver*, you'll be taken on a journey of pain, heartache and suffering, but with a powerful and inspiration message: the ability to overcome. MADD classifies us as victims and survivors, which I strongly disagree with. If we were victims, we wouldn't be able to share our souls with readers in this book. The pain and suffering will never go away, yet we still find a reason to get out of bed—because, we are survivors.

Those of us who are impacted by drunk and drugged driving often get frustrated at the justice system because we feel justice is never served in our cases. True, the laws need to change, but that's only one part of the issue. We, as a society, need to change. I'm not against the consumption of alcohol, I'm just against the use of it when it harms someone, especially when someone is intoxicated behind the wheel of the car. And the notion that "everyone does it" is wrong. Not everyone does it.

By writing our stories, we are no longer *victims*. We are *survivors* because we won't let the person who changed our lives win. Survivors overcome, they adapt, they fight on, even when we don't want to. These stories will touch your soul but—most of all—impact your life by offering readers a firsthand look at what impaired driving does to someone.

If you've been impacted by an impaired driver, I want you to know that those who shared our stories speak for you as well. We know what you have experienced and hopefully can inspire you to share your story to help prevent anyone else from being impacted. We are a community that no one asks to be in, but we have a strong bond with incredible support.

On the day I wrote this foreword, I attended the memorial service of a former student's brother who was killed by a drunk driver. His family now knows the horrific impact of impaired driving. It's time that we as a society make a change. Driving impaired is preventable. How many more need to join the list of us impacted by impaired driving? Can we come together to make our communities safer and prevent impaired driving?

I hope so…I truly hope so.

MICHAEL GERSHE
Founder, The Magic of Life, Inc
www.themagicoflife.org
info@themagicoflife.org

BY LYNDA CHELDELIN FELL

# PREFACE

Years ago when I was an EMT, I was on the scene of a head-on collision between two drunk drivers. It happened on a highway near a rural high school, and the scene was brutal. Both drivers had already gotten out of their vehicles and were walking around, but the body of a large dog was laying just outside the driver's door and a badly injured teenage girl was trapped inside.

I was small enough that I could climb into the crushed car to tend to the girl. My young patient's name was Kaitlyn, and I had never seen someone with so much physical trauma and still breathing. The scene was chaotic. While firefighters used the jaws of life to cut through the mangled metal, I tried to immobilize Kaitlyn's head and keep her calm through the noise.

Once extricated, her injuries were too severe to keep her cervical spine aligned on the backboard using a traditional strap. I had to remain in a hunched position to immobilize her head as she was loaded into the medic unit, her clothing cut off, advanced life support started, and even while the trauma team took over tending to her injuries in the hospital.

This entire time I spoke softly into Kaitlyn's ear, reassuring her I wouldn't leave her side. At one point she opened her eyes, looked directly into mine, and asked if her teeth were okay. She smiled for me so I could get a good look. Her teeth were perfect. But the rest of her body was grotesque—and broken beyond repair.

I gently reassured Kaitlyn that her teeth were beautiful. My words were the last she would ever hear.

The damage done by two drunk drivers was irreversible: my beautiful teen patient died. Both drunk drivers lived.

It's been nearly 15 years since that night, and I've been on many other memorable incidents but I've never forgotten Kaitlyn.

I've never forgotten her because I've never seen the human body so badly injured, before or since.

I've never forgotten her because her teeth were perfect, but the rest of her body was beyond repair.

I've never forgotten her because Kaitlyn—a beautiful teen girl on the cusp of life—died.

And two drunk drivers lived.

I share this story with you because it reveals a different kind of impact from the stories contained in this book. Kaitlyn's injuries—the result of two drunk drivers—were so severe, the sight of her badly damaged body will stay with me for life.

The reason for sharing our stories is to raise awareness and offer comfort to those who share our path. If you or someone you love has been hit by an impaired driver, the following true stories are written by people who know exactly how you feel. Although no two journeys are identical, we hope you'll find comfort in our stories and the understanding that you aren't truly alone, for we walk ahead, behind, and right beside you.

Wishing you healing and hope from our Grief Diaries village.

*Lynda Cheldelin Fell*

# CHAPTER ONE

# THE BEGINNING

Infinity is a way to describe the incomprehensible to the human mind. In a way, it notates a mystery. That kind of mystery exists in relationships. A lifetime is not enough to know someone else. It provides a brief glimpse. -SIMON MCBURNEY

Every journey is as unique as a fingerprint. To fully appreciate the different perspectives, it is helpful to understand the journeys. In this chapter, each writer shares that very moment when their world was impacted by an impaired driver to help you understand when life as they knew it ended and a new one began.

\*

JESSICA WEYER BENTLEY
Jessica was 5 when her 24-year-old father
Robert was killed by a drunk driver in 1979

When I allow my mind to wonder back to this very dark time my first memory was not the day my father was killed, but the week before on my birthday. I was turning five on September 9, 1979. I remember being so excited running through the house, seeing my cake in the kitchen. I was running down the hall with bounding energy and noticed that our hall closet door was cracked open just slightly. I remember peering inside the closet and seeing gifts I just knew were for my birthday. I remember being so happy because they were from my father. I don't know how I remember this, but I remember a doll and a teddy bear were waiting for me in there. I remember feeling so loved because he had sent me presents. You see, my world at five had already been turned upside down. My parents divorced, my mother remarried and moved me a state away from everything I had known. That included my father and, though I didn't know it at the time, my world a week from then was going to grow quite dark. But for this moment in time, before everything tilted upside down and went gray, I remember being happy and it is the last untainted memory I own. What comes next has taken me down a very dark thirty-year road.

Due to the trauma, my memories are minimal. I've blocked most of my childhood due to the grief, depression, insomnia, and nightmares. I do not remember much from that time in my life. But there is one memory that comes into a painful and sharp focus; a memory that has been in my nightmares all of my life, and the only true memory I have of my father. It haunts me to this day, and I still have difficulty sleeping with fear that this memory will enter my nightmares again, just as it has so many times before.

I remember in great detail the little white house my mother and stepfather drove up to. We walked up a small set of concrete steps under a black and white awning. As we entered the oak and glass double doors, I caught a whiff of a smell I now dread: the scent of all the funeral flowers. Dad was quite young when he was killed so his death was very tragic to our community. He was a police officer who was still in his twenties, so the number of flowers and people filled the room to the rafters. It was overwhelming just walking into that little room with literally standing room only.

I didn't understand at the time why so many people were crying or why they were staring somberly at me, but even as a young child I knew those people understood something I did not. It was then, with everyone looking on, that I saw my father. It was the first time in months.

We were making our way through the tiny room when we passed by where he was lying. I looked closely at his face. I was puzzled as to why he was in this big black box. I do recall being excited to see him but confused as to why he was sleeping in front of all of those people. I remember wondering why my daddy refused to open his eyes and talk to me. He was not reaching for me or moving at all. I remember thinking that he didn't look like himself. It was then when my five-year-old brain realized that something was terribly wrong. I had sudden fear and complete shock. As the shock hit me, I started crying for him and began to scream. I was kicking as hard as I could trying to get loose from my mother's grip. I had to be restrained. Everyone was glaring at me with deep concern and alarm. It was then that my family made the decision to remove me from the funeral home. That was the last time I saw my father. This image has haunted my nightmares for over thirty years. I still cannot go inside that funeral home without panic rising in me. It turned my life black.

Robert Lyle Weyer was twenty-four years old on September 16, 1979. Around 2 a.m. he was trying to repair his car outside the Sunset Supper Club, a small bar along State Route 309 in Kenton, Ohio. While working on his car, a drunk driver's pickup truck left the roadway and hit my father, pinning him against the front of his own car. The driver tried to flee but was stopped at the scene by witnesses. The injuries that Dad suffered were traumatic and he had extensive hemorrhaging.

Near the site of the crash was a local hospital, and witnesses ran to get help. At that time Life Flight was unavailable so my father was stabilized and transported by ambulance from Kenton to The Ohio State University in Columbus, two hours away. For the next twelve hours, physicians fought to save my father but unfortunately the damage was too extensive and he left this world.

While my father lay dying on the road in the dark, early hours of that morning, I was sleeping in my little bed. I never got to say goodbye. The permanent decision made by a drunk driver to get behind the wheel of that pickup truck flung me into years of grieving imprisonment. The light of the world dimmed greatly for me that day. It was permanent. It was a choice, and his death was one hundred percent preventable.

Since that horrific moment of seeing my father unrecognizable in his casket, I have suffered years of nightmares, insomnia, and flashbacks. From the age of five to age eighteen, it was truly touch and go with my life. Depression was a constant companion. When I met my husband in high school, my world brightened for the first time. The depression lessened but the trauma and PTSD is a permanent reminder. I would never wish for my children to know the lack of protection that losing a parent brings.

As a child, I would focus on my loss and the unfair situation I found myself in. I fixated on how traumatic my life was without Dad, but after all of this time, I now realize the true horror of it all. As a mother of two beautiful children, I cannot imagine the agony he went through and the sheer terror he felt knowing that he was leaving behind his defenseless child. How frightened he must have been, and how worried he must have been knowing he would not be here to guide or love me. A father's greatest fear is to be unable to protect his daughter from the world. That bond is the greatest I have ever seen, and now having children of my own, I can fully imagine his torture. It is unfathomable.

It has taken years of reflection, prayer, crying, volunteering, and speaking about this tragedy to others to heal the wounds and profound grief I have suffered having my father ripped from me. It has not been easy, but I can say that I have found a place of peace. But that peace has not stopped the chronic nightmares, flashbacks, insomnia, and panic which are all part of the PTSD.

Let me close by saying the true tragedy is that we all lost a good man on that road; a young man full of possibilities and life. A man who contributed to his community and his family. We lost his humor, his laughter, his joy, and his love. We all lose, and the loss is not necessary. That is the greatest tragedy. Impaired driving crashes are preventable. It just takes making the simple decision to find another way home. Robert Weyer was just a kid on that road, alone, and dying with so much potential. The true tragedy of our story is that drunk driving deaths did not stop with my dad. They continue to happen every day around the clock, creating more unnecessary suffering.

As fate would have it, on Labor Day 2016, my husband, son, and I were hit by a drunk driver in Portsmouth, Ohio. We were lucky, although my husband is recovering from his injuries. The tragedy continues. But we will prevail and with great tragedy comes strength. I will use every ounce of strength I have to fight this until my breath ceases and my father is once again before me.

\*

SHANNON BOOS
Shannon was 20 when her 21-year-old brother
Kevin was killed by a drunk driver in 2015

If I had to describe Kevin in one word, it would be "dedicated," and I would use that word in many different ways. He was dedicated to his job and his future. Kevin did have a tough time finding his passion and what he wanted to do with his life for a couple of years. However, when he found it, he was unstoppable. His passion for music was indescribable. He was constantly working on it, talking about it, and promoting it. He was so determined to make a future out of it that he would do anything to get there. He even dedicated one whole summer to doing chores and yardwork for our grandmother to make enough money to buy his own keyboard.

While he was working on his music, Kevin had a job as a busboy. To most, this would be a low-end lame job that would be seen as shameful or not really something to talk about. Not Kevin. He talked about that place as if he worked for the president of the United States. He loved his job, and I'm not sure that love is even a strong enough word to describe it. He was always so excited to go to work, bus tables, make friends, and get to know the customers. I fondly remember him "complaining" that he had to go to work, but he always had his signature smirk on his face when he was getting ready to leave. We never found out what was so special about that restaurant, but seeing him happy with something so simple was all that mattered. He was so easily excitable and driven, and those were two of my favorite characteristics about him.

Kevin was so dedicated to his family and his friends. I know it is pretty typical for someone to say that his or her loved one who passed was the best person there was, and in my case I say it with confidence. Kevin was so loving, so understanding, and so patient. He wasn't perfect, but he was as close as it gets. There were many people who wouldn't be given a second glance by most, but he never gave up on them. A lot of people gave up on me, but he never left my side. And for that, I am forever grateful to him.

He spent two years in Tallahassee, Florida, studying at Florida State University pursuing a music degree. He loved the school, the Seminoles, the city, the atmosphere. If it was related to FSU, he was all about it. He spent one year as the president of Epsilon Sigma Alpha, which is a co-ed service fraternity. He constantly attended and ran community service events, raising money, supporting the homeless, and doing all kinds of incredible things that the average person would never do.

I was Kevin's protector. Though sixteen months younger than him, I took the older sister role. He was very shy, sensitive, and quiet. My parents even had him tested for autism but doctors couldn't diagnose him with it. I was always so worried about him, even while we were in college together. However as soon as he left high school, he grew into his own and became a confident, strong man. His successes were incredible in the short time he was at FSU, and he worked so hard toward his dreams.

Unfortunately Kevin didn't get into the music program at FSU, for reasons we will never know. And although we all knew he was so heartbroken, he again made something great out of it. He moved home to southern Florida and in with our brother Jeffrey. He got a job as a busboy and started to really work on his music. Most would have given up on their passion due to rejection, but Kevin used it to fuel himself to work even harder. Every single day he was working on his music, making money on the side, and had that big grin on his face no matter what life threw at him.

On the weekend of September 6, 2015, Kevin and a few friends traveled up to Florida State to spend Labor Day Weekend with friends. He was so excited to see everyone again, to attend a football game, and to have fun in his favorite city. That Sunday night, Kevin and his three friends Morgan, Vincenzo, and Niko, left a friend's apartment to pick up some food. What they didn't know was that someone had made the selfish, disgusting decision to get behind the wheel after too much to drink. At 9:15 p.m. Kevin and his two friends, Vincenzo and Morgan, were all killed by a drunk driver. That's when our world stopped.

*

TIFFANY COLSON
Tiffany was 30 when she was
hit by a drunk driver in 2011

On March 23, 2011, I was hit head-on by a drunk driver. The day started out normal and I was eager to go to work. My best friend was going to be married in a couple of weeks, and I needed to make some money to buy a dress. I was a delivery driver for a well-known pizza franchise. I got to work at 5 p.m. that Wednesday night. It was slow, so when an order came up, I was ready to take it. The address was nearby. I delivered the pizza and was on my way back to the store. I was in the turn lane waiting to make a left-hand turn. There was a lot of traffic in our small town, so I had to wait a few minutes before I could turn. While sitting there in the turn lane, I noticed an oncoming truck traveling partway in the turn lane. The speed limit is 55 on this road, so he was going very fast. I watched him and thought to myself "Wow. He's going too fast to make that turn." I thought he was going to turn onto the road to my right, but then I realized he wasn't going to turn.

From that point on, everything seemed to slow down. I sat up straight and looked in my side mirror to see if I could pull out, but there were too many cars. I then took a deep breath and gripped the steering wheel. I do not know why, but I chose to stare at his bumper as he hit me at full speed. The police have no idea how fast he was going because he didn't apply his brakes. We collided, driver side to driver side. His truck flipped and my car spun. I was driving a 1999 Saturn SL1 and he was in a Chevy Silverado.

He was not wearing a seatbelt and was thrown through the back window. I was wearing a seatbelt but became trapped in my car. My feet were trapped. It seemed to happen all at once. I took off my seatbelt and tried to turn off the car and open the door but realized I couldn't get out. I was able to wiggle out my right foot but my left foot wouldn't move. I tried to reach for my cellphone but it was gone. I began screaming as loud as I could.

I honestly thought that no one would stop and help me. Luckily, a man ran over and took charge of the scene. Later I found out that he was a retired sheriff who had been across the street at the drive-in having dinner with his wife. They were leaving and were almost hit in the wreck. Another man stopped to help, and he was exactly who I needed at that moment. I did not immediately recognize him, but he was a regular customer of mine. He held my hand the entire time, even when the fire department was cutting me out of the car. They put a jacket over him while he laid on the floorboard and held my hand. I later found out that he was driving drunk that night and almost didn't stop to help. It still feels odd that a drunk driver tried to kill me and another one stopped to help.

It took about an hour from the time of the wreck until I arrived at the hospital. My face was bloody but I was hopped up on adrenaline. I don't think I realized how bad my feet were at the time. I asked the good Samaritans at the scene of the wreck how the other driver was, but they told me not to worry about it. I thought maybe that meant the driver was okay. I was panicked and worried about myself. When the retired sheriff first ran out to stop traffic, he checked on the other driver but thought he was dead. He had no pulse and looked really bad. The retired sheriff then came running when he heard me screaming. The cops came to the emergency room with multiple paper bags filled with prescriptions, bottles of alcohol, and cans of beer that they had recovered from the scene of the wreck. They began asking me questions and I thought that was odd, so I asked them how the other driver was. That's when they told me that the other driver was drunk and may not make it.

I was mad. I was angry. I was *hot*. I grew up in a very dysfunctional family and the main culprit was alcohol. I had too many drunks and too much violence in my childhood. I took this very personally. It was a slap in the face. I ended up with a shattered left foot and significant tissue and muscle damage on my right foot. My knees had no skin, and I was cut from head to toe from the glass. The airbag had busted my nose, so there was blood all over my face, and I had two black eyes. The drunk driver lived, but he has brain damage from the skull fracture that resulted from when his head slammed into the pavement. I have healed but I cannot be on my feet for more than a few hours or it hurts and my feet swell up. I still have scars and bruises after five years. The emotional bruises will last forever.

*

WENDY DAVIDSON
Wendy was 47 when her 28-year-old son
Chuck was killed by a drunk driver in 2016

September 9, 2016, was a normal day for me and for my son Chuck. He is the oldest of my five children. He is, or was, a bartender for a popular pizza restaurant in Delaware. He worked summers at the beach to earn extra money because he and his younger brother were planning to buy a house together.

In the early morning hours of September 10, Chuck was heading home after beach bartending all night. Around 12:30 a.m., he stopped to get a cup of coffee and text his girlfriend, Stephanie, to let her know where he was and that, funnily, a car identical to his was parked in the store's parking lot. He continued traveling home to Dover, which is thirty to forty-five minutes from the beach. While stopped at a light, he texted Stephanie again to let her know that he missed her. That was the last text she would ever receive from Chuck.

Witnesses called the police department at 12:50 a.m. to report an intoxicated driver. He had almost hit another motorist after doing donuts on the side of the highway, forcing that driver onto the wrong side of the road. Police were dispatched to find the offender but at 1:12 a.m., the drunk driver hit my son's car head-on. According to the police, it appeared that Chuck tried to steer out of the way, but the left side of the drunk driver's Mercedes-Benz hit the left side of Chuck's 1999 Volkswagen Passat. Chuck's car flipped onto its hood and slid off the road into the woods. My son died instantly. His death certificate cites multiple blunt force traumas as the cause of death, and the newspaper stated that he was wearing his seatbelt.

The police went to my son's residence and told my other two children, Chuck's younger siblings Chris and Caity, that their brother was dead. Chris and Caity then had the unfortunate task of driving to their father's home to inform him of the tragedy.

I received a phone call from Chuck's dad at 5:32 a.m. I immediately knew something was wrong. I was afraid to pick up the phone, and sometimes I wish I hadn't. He was obviously upset, and all I could do was scream at him, "Which one? Which one?" I wanted to know immediately which of my children was in trouble. He said to me, sobbing, that Chucky was killed by a drunk driver. The only word that I could muster was, "No... No....No..." The word "no" turned into a yell, and then became a scream, and then became the darkest day of my life.

My husband ran downstairs and woke my youngest son and asked him to talk to his dad on the phone. All I could do was sob. When disaster strikes and you attempt to sort what was just said to you, you begin asking yourself questions — the why, the what, the where. What exactly happened? Was he scared? Did he suffer? Where was the accident exactly? What color was the car? Some questions seem very inconsequential and others meaningful, but they all come swarming into your mind at once. We then had to drive to my youngest daughter Carly's house to inform her of the horrific news. I realized that I had more than one cross to bear. Not only am I suffering the loss of Chuck, but I have to watch my children suffer as well.

My husband, two of my children, and I spent that day just being close to each other. We planned to travel to Dover the following morning. I really didn't want to delay the three-hour drive, but it was necessary to arrange for care of the animals on our farm. It was one of those days when you really didn't have to say anything; we were all completely and utterly devastated. It was surreal. You can't comprehend the loss, nor the numbness that follows. You can't fathom, understand, or want to know just how final death is until you lose a child. As anyone will tell you, it's just not the right order of things. You can hear or see fleeting images of faces of those who have died in an accident like this one when they get reported on the local news, and you think "How sad," but it will not bear any meaning for you until it happens to you. I've become hypersensitive to hearing or reading about a death involving a drunk driver, whereas before I never really registered it, sadly. I am guilty of it, and feel ashamed. In my opinion, death by drunk driver is one of the most preventable deaths. It should never happen, and yet it does happen unnecessarily every single day. It's selfish. It's like playing Russian roulette with a car.

It's been just under two months since Chuck's death as of this writing. We honored his wishes and cremated him, and shared his ashes because each family member has a memorial they'd like to do in remembrance of Chuck. His service was standing room only. It's true that you really never know the impact you have on a person's life until you are gone, and this was obvious in my son's case.

My family struggles with the loss of Chuck every day. He was so vibrant and fun. He loved music, played guitar, loved concerts and enjoyed life every moment. Of course he had struggles, but he was always positive. He had only one college semester left before graduation, and was already scheduled for fall classes. He was just a few short weeks away from finishing his undergraduate degree, after eight years of balancing work and school.

It's a loss we will never get over. It's a loss that we now have to learn to live with. There are so many constant reminders. It could be a smell in the air, a mannerism by one of my other children, a song on the radio. Even a simple phrase can make your heart fill with grief. It's so unbearable that it actually physically hurts. You become numb and what you once thought was important no longer has any significance. I have become a statistic, but I am also a grieving mother who has lost her baby. The effects are everlasting, and trying to find peace seems like a daunting task.

*

BILL DOWNS
Bill's 21-year-old son Brad, 19-year-old daughter-in-law<br>Samantha, and 24-year-old family friend Chris<br>were killed by a drunk/drugged driver in 2007

I remember that night like it was last night. My Saturday nights and Cruising the Coast classic cars weekend will never be the same. October 6, 2007, started out like any other day. I was working part-time as a laundromat attendant and was scheduled to work that night. Before I left for work, I told my son Brad and his wife of three months, Samantha, that I loved them and told them to be careful if they went out that night because of the extra traffic on the coast due to the classic cars and crowds. I got in my car and headed to work.

Chris was a young man whom the kids brought home with them when they moved home. My wife Julie and I grew to love Chris as a son in the time he also lived with us. When I got to work Chris was headed home from Jackson, Mississippi, after his girlfriend broke his heart. He called me to get directions on how to get home. When Chris got home, his frame of mind was not very good. Brad and Samantha decided to take Chris to the car races to get his mind off his broken heart, especially since Chris was willing to pay for it. The weather that night was partly cloudy and had been

13

misting off and on, and the race was canceled. The kids decided to go to the movies instead so they drove home in Chris' truck and then changed into Brad's car. Brad wanted to take his car because he had bought this car himself, and it was his dream car.

Chris called as they headed to the movies at 8:50 p.m. I told him I loved him, and reminded them to be careful on the roads. I told him the same thing I had told Brad and Samantha: there were more vehicles on the road because of the Cruising the Coast club along the coast. I warned him that there would be partying and drinking while driving. He said "Love ya, Dad," and hung up.

When I got off work that night, I called Julie and told her I was on my way home. When I got about half way, I came upon a roadblock, and traffic was being detoured. I called Julie and told her I would be late because of a horrific crash involving multiple cars. I told her it was very bad, I had never seen so many emergency vehicles and flashing lights which lit the whole night sky. Because of a large curve on a hill, this was a spot of many crashes. Julie said she would call the kids to warn them of the detour when they headed home. When I reached the other side of the roadblock, Julie called and said she couldn't get the kids on the phone. She asked me to turn around and go back to the roadblock, while she continued to try to reach the kids. I called Julie's brother and asked him to take her keys and not to let her leave until I knew what had happened. I then turned around and drove back to the roadblock.

When I reached the roadblock, an officer told me to go home. I turned around to leave the scene when Julie called again and said she still couldn't reach the kids. I promised her I wouldn't leave until I found something out, but this time the officers threatened to arrest me if I didn't leave.

Meanwhile, Julie called dispatch and the hospital trying to find out details about who was involved in the crash. The hospital confirmed that two victims had been taken to the emergency room, so I headed toward the hospital. When I arrived, I began trying to find out the identity of the victims while Julie and her sisters were on the phone trying to find out the same information. I asked the nurse if she knew who the victims were. While she was checking for me, I got the phone call that no father ever wants to get. Julie called with the news that Brad and Samantha had been involved in that car crash, and didn't survive. Her words still ring loud in my ears. "Bill, our baby is gone! All three are gone! They were killed instantly." I fell to my knees, crying out. My world had just come to an end.

The coroner came to the hospital lobby to console me. He took me into the back of the emergency room and asked if I could identify Chris' body. He said that the driver of the other vehicle was also killed; she was impaired and hit the kids head on at eighty miles per hour. I walked into the room where they had Chris, and my eyes filled with tears as I gazed at the young man I had loved as a son. To see him like this was more than I could bear. My life as I knew it was gone.

*

JULIE DOWNS<br/>
Julie's 21-year-old son Brad, 19-year-old daughter-in-law<br/>
Samantha, and 24-year-old family friend Chris<br/>
were killed by a drunk/drugged driver in 2007

I still hear the words ringing in my ears, "Yes, ma'am, I believe your son is dead," as I recall that tragic night. My son Brad and his bride Samantha had been married for three and a half months and were living with my husband, Bill, and I and our daughter, Cynthia. The year before, Brad brought home a young man who needed a place to stay so he wouldn't be homeless. Chris became a part of our family.

As the kids were sitting around the house on October 6, 2007, they decided to go to the car races. They left the house only to return forty-five minutes later because the rain had caused the races to be canceled. They were disappointed but they were not going to let the rain damper their Saturday night so they decided to go to the movies. As they prepared to leave, Chris leaned down and hugged me and told me that he loved me as I was sitting at my computer. Brad was standing behind him and Chris swatted him in the stomach and told him to give me a hug. Brad playfully jumped backward and said, "I'm not going to hug her," as we all laughed. I told them to go and have fun. As Samantha passed by, we smiled at each other and I told her how pretty she looked.

As Brad was going out the door, he stopped and called my name, "Mom." I looked around the corner and he said, "I love you, see you when we get back." I told him to be careful and to have a good time and that I loved him also. I never dreamed that it was going to be the last time I would see my son, my kids, alive.

An hour later, Bill called to let me know he would be late because of a detour around a roadblock at the scene of a car crash. My maternal instinct kicked in and I told him I would call the kids to make sure they were okay, and to tell them to avoid that area on their way home. Bill said both sides of the highway was closed, and the night sky was brightly lit from all the emergency vehicles.

I first called Brad but he didn't answer his phone, which wasn't unusual when he was at the movies. I then called Samantha, and when she didn't answer I started to panic. Samantha always answered her phone. I then called Chris, but no answer. I knew then that they were involved in that crash.

I immediately called Bill and told him to go back to the roadblock and find the kids. I was going to get in my car and head that way but Bill, fearing the worst, told me to stay put until he found something out. To ensure I didn't try to leave, he called my brother, Alan, to come over and take my keys.

I paced the floor, calling Brad over and over again. My two sisters, Susan and Sandy, heard what was going on and before I knew it, they were there with me and the four of us called everyone we could think of. We kept in touch with Bill, who was going from one side of the roadblock to the other trying to get through. He even raced to the movie theater praying he would find Brad's car parked there, but that was not the case. I called the local hospital and was told that two of the victims from the crash were there. I called Bill with the news and he headed to the hospital.

As I hung up the phone I heard my brother on his phone talking to who I thought was dispatch with the Highway Patrol. I grabbed the phone away from him and said, "Hello, this is Julie Downs." The voice on the other end said, "Mrs. Downs, this is Gary Hargrove, the coroner for Harrison County." I knew if I was talking to the coroner then someone was dead. He asked me what Chris looked like. In between answering him and trying to breathe, I kept screaming, "IS MY SON DEAD?" After what seemed like forever he said, "Yes, ma'am. I believe he is."

I threw down the phone and fell to my knees and wailed like an animal. "Not my son! These things happen to other people, not to me. Noooo, not my son!" I struggled to my feet and got into the passenger side of my car, screaming for someone to take me to the hospital. My sister jumped in, and we drove down the road praying we would wake up from the nightmare.

I called Bill. He was at the hospital trying to find out details about the victims, and I didn't want a stranger to be the one to tell him the news that would destroy him. Bill answered the phone. I said, "Bill. Bill, your baby is gone! All three of them are gone!" When I arrived at the hospital the coroner was there with Bill. We were taken into a small room where he told us that the kids had been killed by a drunk driver. He said she had crossed over into Brad's lane, hitting them head-on, killing Brad and Samantha instantly. Because Chris had a slight heartbeat, he was transported to the hospital but died on the way. He was one of the victims at the hospital. Brad and Samantha went straight to the funeral home. We were assured that they did not suffer. I guess if your child had to die, you would want them not to have suffered. But being told they were dead is not what we wanted to hear.

The coroner said that if the kids had been delayed by just one or two seconds, the drunk driver would have crossed over and hit the ditch instead of them. When the coroner said that, all I could think about was the hug I passed up as Brad was leaving the house. If I had insisted on that hug instead of telling them to go and have fun, my kids might still be alive.

*

MICHAEL GERSHE
Michael was 8-weeks-old when his 28-year-old
mother Barbara was killed by a drunk driver in 1970

On September 19, 1970, almost eight weeks after I was born, my twenty-nine-year-old father, Martin, was driving us home from visiting friends out on Long Island. My three-year-old brother, Jeff, was in the backseat sleeping. My twenty-eight-year-old mother, Barbara, was sitting in the front middle seat next to my father. I was in a little baby carrier next to my mother and the passenger door for the drive home. Approximately around 11 p.m., at the intersection of Route 45 and New Hempstead Road in Spring Valley, New York, our lives were changed by a drunk driver.

As we proceeded through the green light, a drunk driver plowed through the intersection and crashed into our car. The force of the impact was so loud that it woke people in nearby homes. My father was knocked unconscious and doesn't remember seeing the bright lights of the car that hit us. Our car was pushed into a pole that split the front end all the way to the dashboard. It was completely totaled.

An ambulance arrived about twenty minutes after the crash. First responders found my father, brother, and mother, but couldn't find me because I wasn't making any noise in the twisted metal. It took nearly fifteen minutes before I was finally discovered sandwiched between the dashboard and front passenger door.

When my father came to, he cried out, "Where is my baby? Where is my baby?" He doesn't remember if it was a first responder or one of the neighbors who had wrapped me in either a coat or blanket. The patrolman on the scene requested a surgeon be on standby at Ramapo General Hospital. About forty minutes after the crash, an ambulance was finally transporting us to the hospital.

My brother miraculously did not have a scratch on him, but my father needed stitches. I wasn't so lucky. Nearly every bone in my body was broken. My skull was fractured and my injuries were too severe so I was airlifted to a different hospital. My uncle Charlie told me years later that I had no neck, as it was just my head sitting on top of my shoulders. My father often said that no one knew how I survived such severe injuries. My mother, Barbara, was rushed to the hospital and into surgery. They said that when the crash happened, she likely hit her head on either the dashboard or the rearview mirror.

Per the police report, the drunk driver and his friends lied at the scene about who was driving. It turns out that the drunk driver's license had been revoked and he wasn't even supposed to be driving. The patrolman documented a "very strong smell of alcoholic beverage on his breath and that his eyes were bloodshot, his speech was very slurred." Around 2 a.m. after questioning him at the hospital, the drunk driver finally admitted that he was behind the wheel of the car. His blood was taken at 2:54 a.m. and registered a blood alcohol content of .10 nearly four hours after crashing into our car.

My mother, who was only twenty-eight years old, died the morning of September 20, 1970, hours after the drunk driver who was driving with a revoked license, crashed into us. As lucky as I am to be alive, I'm forty-six years old and never got to know my mother because of an impaired driver.

*

ANNETTE HANKS
Annette was 39 when she and her husband and their
13-month-old granddaughter were hit by a drunk driver in 2013

My husband, Wyatt, and I had the pleasure of babysitting our thirteen-month-old granddaughter Adilyn on August 19, 2013. We had some errands to run in town, so we hopped into the van and headed out. Adilyn loved music and singing so we always had fun in the car. When we were done with our errands we began to drive home. Wyatt was driving, I was in the passenger seat, and Adilyn was in the rear passenger seat directly behind me. Our town had recently installed lighted signs at pedestrian crossings, and as we were driving down Broadway Avenue one of the crosswalks began to blink. My husband slowed and came to a stop and so did the car next to us. A few months prior I had been rear-ended by a vehicle, so I was very leery of sitting in the road at a stop. I looked in my side mirror to see what was behind us and saw a black car a few blocks behind. I continued to watch as this car kept getting closer, and closer, and closer, until I yelled. He slammed into us at over 40 miles per hour. He hit us so hard that his engine block dug an eighteen-inch gouge in the roadway. The sounds, smells, and sights are things I'll never forget.

Wyatt and I both immediately went to Adilyn. She was knocked unconscious. The right side of her head and her right eye were already swelling and blue. She looked dead. We knew to keep her in her car seat. I crawled through the rubble and grabbed her head to keep it steady until the ambulance could get there. By God's perfect timing, He placed a police officer named Kohl across the street at a business less than a minute before the crash. He was there immediately.

At one point, Adilyn began to have a seizure and her eyes rolled back in her head. That was the first sign of life I saw in her. I was praying and begging God not to take her.

After what seemed like an eternity, the ambulance got there and they took Adilyn out of our van and into the ambulance. I was taken to the hospital by another police officer. I paced and paced waiting for the ambulance to get there. When they did, they wheeled her in and she was half crying half whimpering, still unconscious. That was the greatest noise in the whole world! Once they got her stable, they allowed me to go back with her. Moments later, the emergency room doors open and my daughter Marque walks in with a look of sheer terror on her face. My heart was crushed so hard because it was our responsibility to keep her precious baby girl safe, but we failed.

Adilyn underwent x-rays and CT scans which revealed two orbital skull fractures and bleeding in her brain. She would have to be airlifted to Harborview Medical Center, a level one trauma unit in Seattle. At this point Adilyn still hadn't regained consciousness. She was able to fuss and whimper, but nothing else. The flight crew swiftly prepared Adilyn and Marque and off they went.

Wyatt and I couldn't leave because we hadn't yet been examined by the doctors. I had a possible broken wrist and both of us had extremely hurt necks and backs. We begged doctors to let us leave so we could begin the three-hour drive to Harborview. We didn't know what the outcome was going to be for Adilyn, and we wanted to be with her. They wouldn't let us go.

Eight hours after the crash, we were finally released from the hospital and headed straight for Seattle. When we arrived at the hospital, we sat in waiting room chairs and tried to sleep.

At 7:30 a.m. the next morning, my mother-in-law woke me and said Adilyn was awake. I jumped up so fast and ran to the door of the pediatric intensive care unit. As I peered through the tiny window, Adilyn saw me and tried to stand up in her crib and reach out for me. Crying, I burst through the doors and ran to her. The nurse let me pick Adilyn up and hold her. That was the first moment I saw my beautiful granddaughter alive since the crash. Her right eye was purple and swollen shut, and her entire face was puffy, but she smiled at me and kissed me. I knew she would be okay.

*

RENE LEDFORD
Rene's 25-year-old son Justin Colt
was killed by a drunk driver in 2015

On August 20, 2015, my twenty-five-year-old son Justin Colt and his friend were on his motorcycle on their way to town. Justin made the friend wear his helmet, which saved her life. At 10:38 p.m., a drunk driver ran two stop signs and turned onto a one-way street going the wrong way. He hit my son's motorcycle head-on. Justin Colt was killed instantly and his friend was severely injured. The drunk driver then peeled away from the crash still going the wrong way. He drove nearly three miles until his truck lost a front tire. The drunk driver then stopped other drivers, telling them that he was just involved in an accident and needed to get out of there. They held him until law enforcement arrived.

My son was lying on the road under a sheet at the crash site while the drunk driver was questioned less than three miles away. Law enforcement took him back to the scene, and the drunk driver started asking why they had stopped here at this accident. He was told by law enforcement that he killed the person under the sheet, but he insisted that his crash was somewhere else, not here, and not to show him this. He was taken to jail.

Our son was identified by a judge who knew both my dad and my son. He and two officers came to notify us. They told my dad and mom first. My dad then came busting through our door, but he couldn't talk and my husband kept asking him what was wrong. As I came out of my bedroom I heard my dad say, "Justin was killed on his motorcycle." My husband screamed, "Oh, God. Oh, God," and collapsed into my dad's arms.

I started to gather my stuff to go to the hospital to get my son. I called my youngest daughter, screaming for her to come, not realizing she wasn't yet home from work. When I walked out the door I saw the judge and two officers, and right then I knew we weren't going anywhere. It was almost 1 a.m., and Justin Colt was never out that late. My brother ran into my son's room to see if he was asleep as I kept asking over and over, "Are you sure it's him? He's never out. He's asleep in his room, and a friend borrowed his motorcycle." The judge looked at me with so much sincerity and replied, "I know what Justin looks like. It's him. We got the drunk driver and he's on the way to jail. It happened at 10:38 p.m. and Justin was killed instantly."

I called my oldest daughter, and all I could do was scream and try to tell her to get here now. My husband got on the phone and told her what happened. A few minutes later they pulled up. She still wasn't sure what had happened until she saw all of us crying, and then she knew—Justin Colt was gone.

I asked if I could go see Justin. With compassion, the judge said we would need to have a closed coffin service, but he would make sure Justin Colt would be taken care of after the autopsy.

A week later, on Thursday, August 27, 2015, we buried my son.

*

MELISSA MORIN
Melissa was 30 when she was
hit by a drunk driver in 2013

In November 2013, myself and three friends, Jill, Amy, and Neddi decided to have a girls' night out. It had been years since we had gotten together and had girl time. All of us are mothers, and we all looked forward to seeing each other. I remember it was a cold Saturday, and Jill was working a very long day. We worked together at the same place and when Jill got off work, she then got ready and met me at my house. I will never forget the cold — it was a crackling kind of cold.

We took my car and met Amy and Neddi at a local bar in Indiana. When we left, we decided to ride in Neddi's car because it was bigger than mine, and I wasn't too familiar with Indiana. We went to a couple of different establishments and were having a good time! Around 2 a.m. Jill was ready to go home, so we all got into Neddi's car and left. I remember we were driving down the street and came to a stop sign. When we turned left, I wasn't really paying much attention when all of a sudden I heard Neddi say, "Look at this m#*% f#@;!" And then I heard "Seatbelts! Seatbelts!"

Before I could react I remember an eerie type of quiet, like nothing I've ever experienced before. I looked up, and saw a bright light as I stared at Jill. I remember her head turning in the bright light and as I looked down, I realized I was in midair. I had no clue as to what was happening. It didn't register.

The next thing I remember was screaming that my arm was broken! I didn't know that would be the least of my problems. I then remember asking Jill's aunt and Neddi what had happened. I asked about Jill and got complete silence. Jill's aunt then said that Jill was gone. In my heart, I somehow already knew.

I was in and out of it for almost a week before I was coherent enough to understand what was wrong with me. I had suffered a broken neck, broken back, and fractured my pelvis in two places. I also had an orbital fracture, broken rib, cracked breastbone, and a severe gash on my arm. The doctors couldn't believe I wasn't paralyzed; they said I was a miracle.

For almost a week the doctors didn't know where to start first. I remember my brother sitting by my bed when a doctor came in to do something to my face. I didn't know what was going on, but I remember looking at my brother and crying. My head hurt so bad. I couldn't take the pain so my mom cut my butt-length hair off. When she did, glass fell out. No wonder it hurt so bad!

The week of my thirty-first birthday I underwent three major surgeries, one every other day. First was neck surgery but the anesthesia didn't go well. I was beside myself and scared my mother. Next was back surgery. It was the worst pain I have ever felt in my life! I have never cried for my mother the way I did that day. I laid there with fifty staples in my back. I was given a remote control for morphine to help with pain, and thanked God for prescription drugs.

Next came pelvic surgery. It wasn't as terrible. The back surgery by far was the worst of the three, and it still haunts me. I started physical therapy one week later. I had to learn how to sit up and get into a wheelchair. I fell right over on the first try. They picked me up and I tried again. This second time I stayed up and saw myself in a mirror. I realized then that my forehead had been stitched back on. Nobody told me; they didn't want me to lose it because I was already going through enough. I was really upset. I wish they had told me right away.

I was allowed to leave the hospital after almost three weeks. I couldn't go home because I lived on the third floor. I went to live with my parents instead so they could care for me. I had a home nurse and physical therapist. My physical therapist became my best friend; I looked forward to seeing her every day! The hardest part was not being able to do anything. My son was eleven months old at the time, so it was terribly hard. I couldn't do anything for him, let alone myself. Thank God for my parents, in-laws, and fiancé. He held it together the entire time. He was working sixteen-hour days to make sure the bills were paid (we also work at the same place).

In February, I was finally allowed to go home! I was scared at first. I had to figure out what the new norm was, on top of having the worst anxiety I've ever had in my life! I had to do outpatient physical therapy. That was hard work, plus I now had a therapist I didn't like!

Almost seven months later I went back to work. I probably should have walked away and allowed myself recovery time, both physically and mentally. I didn't know what else to do, I'm a worker! Almost three years later, I'm still working. I'm not sure how much longer though. Simple things are becoming physically too tough. It has affected my relationship in both good and bad ways. My fiancé tries to understand, but gets frustrated because he does the bulk of things, even when it comes to our son. It breaks my heart because sometimes I feel like he doesn't understand and I find myself in tears. My back is fused so I can't even pick up my son, he's too heavy. It's all the little things I can't do that break my heart.

The offender in our case was a twenty-three-year-old habitual DUI offender. He dragged the case on until this year. In April, he took a plea deal and was sentenced to ten years with a revocation of his license for five years after he gets out. In my opinion, that doesn't matter because he shouldn't have been driving when he hit us. He's still going to drive no matter what. He'll do maybe five years. To me, they could never give him enough prison time, but at the end of the day it's not going to fix us or bring Jill back. Her children will suffer forever because of his ignorant and preventable choices. Our lives will be affected forever.

In court, I told the driver I hated him and that I'll never forgive him. I never got to say goodbye to my friend. I will forever cherish our sixteen years of friendship.

Missing you always, Miss Jilly Jill. And forever friends with Amy and Neddi. At the end of the day, all we have is each other.

*

LINDA PAULSON
Linda was 40 when her husband and their two
young sons were killed by a drunk driver in 2003

Around 11 a.m. on July 12, 2003, my husband and I, our two young boys, ages ten and eight, and our golden retriever were going on a family picnic when we were hit by a drunk driver. My husband, both our sons and our dog were all killed instantly. The drunk driver, who was three and a half times over the legal limit, also died. My life was forever changed that day and continues to be a struggle.

*

NICOLE RAMOS
Nicole was 32 when she and her two
children were hit by a drunk driver in 2013

I was born and raised in southern California. I grew up with two brothers in the same house, and have three more brothers and two sisters from my father's side. I grew up with all boys in our neighborhood. We played football, stickball, cops and robbers, and rode our bikes all over town. I loved to swim in our pool, body surf in the ocean, and jump on our trampoline.

My stepdad got me interested in softball at the age of five. I fell in love with the sport and bonded with my female teammates. I played softball for fifteen years. After graduating from college, I decided I wasn't ready to give it up. I started coaching at the college level and then began to study the game and pursue my master's degree. When I got pregnant with my second child, I decided to leave the college scene and stay closer to home.

With one daughter who was active in competitive soccer and softball and another on the way, I couldn't divide my time between work and family. My daughter Audrey, my son Elijah, and I moved fifteen miles away to get a fresh start. I began teaching at the junior high and coached at the high school. We bought into the "Friday Night Lights" culture at Permian High School in Odessa, Texas, and was immediately welcomed to the Mojo family. We went to the college, junior high, and high school volleyball, basketball, football and softball games. Our family was involved in athletics all day, every day. My husband is a college softball coach, so we supported his team and all their events too.

When my daughter Audrey was going into junior high and my son Elijah was entering Pre-K, they were both going to be involved in sports year-round. Most of our days consisted of practice, travel, and games. I decided it was again time to make a shift in my profession so I could watch my children grow. I left the junior high and high school positions to teach Pre-K. It was a huge difference from college and high school, but I loved spending time with the little ones. I taught Pre-K at our church for five years.

Summers consisted of visiting family and family vacation with all the kids, including my three stepchildren. We would load up into our Suburban and travel to a national park, camp, go to a theme park, or to the beach. Our five children looked forward to hiking, swimming, and horseback riding, exploring and making new memories together. Our busy schedules keep us from all being together at the same time, so we really looked forward to summer vacations and creating memories together.

In mid-October, our family was stretched in all different directions. My husband and I coached a 14-U traveling softball team that had just played in a Think Pink tournament. We paid off our Suburban the month before and spent our first month without a car payment buying a new car stereo. I remember how exciting it was to try out the Bluetooth feature and all the extras it offered. The old stereo shorted out after a glass of sweet tea fell out of the cup holder, soaking the stereo. The buttons stuck and we couldn't change channels or it would just scan until we turned it off. Audrey became the permanent DJ with her auxiliary cord and iPod.

She was toward the end of her junior high volleyball season and preparing for the all-city tournament. Elijah was enjoying his first season of flag football by mimicking what the Permian boys do on Friday nights. My husband Tommy had just finished fall scrimmages and started the recruiting season. I was wrapping up our Red Ribbon Week celebration on campus and preparing for Halloween by transitioning my door decorations to spiders, candy corn, and monsters.

After the school bell rang on Friday, October 25, we rushed from academic life to the weekend athletic life. I picked up Elijah and then Audrey from school. Tommy was in Las Vegas recruiting prospective student-athletes for the next academic year. When we made it home, Audrey got all dressed up in her best outfit to attend her first Halloween party. I was hesitant to let her go because she had a volleyball tournament, and there was going to be a large group of kids from her school. She ended up going, but we had to lay down the law on what time she would be home. After dropping Audrey off around 7 p.m., Elijah and I went to Target to shop for his Halloween costume, candy, and pumpkins. When we returned home, he tried on his Wolverine costume and I took a picture to post on Instagram and Facebook for the family to see.

Around 9 p.m., Elijah was getting sleepy so he changed into his pajamas but I told him he couldn't go to sleep because we still had to pick up Audrey. About 9:30, Audrey asked if she could stay until 10:15. I told her no because Eli was getting cranky and 10 p.m. was our agreement. Elijah was in his pajamas and fell asleep in the Suburban before we were halfway to Audrey's friend's house.

The house was way out in the country. It was dark but I could see about fifty kids on the front lawn waiting for their parents. I couldn't tell if Audrey was outside so I parked, opened the door and went around the backside of the Suburban, but then I saw the interior lights come on and Audrey climbing into the passenger seat. I got back in, looked in the back to check on Elijah, put my seatbelt on, and put the Suburban in drive.

Audrey began telling me about all the drama that happened at the party, flipping through her phone while sharing all the details. I was not familiar with the area but could see a store sign on the street I needed. As I turned left at the stop sign, I noticed that the speed limit was high and figured I must be on the highway. I started to accelerate and checked my approximation to the store so I could make another left turn to head back to town. Just then I saw a black Lincoln coming toward us and then, to my surprise, a small gold Kia Optima moved onto the shoulder like it was going to pass the Lincoln. What an idiot, I thought to myself. The Kia then hit the rear corner of the Lincoln, sending it into a spin and then I saw its headlights pointing directly at our windshield. I yelled, "Oh!" and then probably profanity which caught my daughter's attention. As she looked up, I heard the deafening sound of crumpling metal. Then came absolute silence.

Everything went black, and I accepted death right then and there. I felt at peace, but then noticed a white fleck and followed it across my field of vision. Black then became brown, and the noise returned. Over and over again our Suburban rolled until landing in a roadside ditch. Dust and smoke filled the car, and so did the smell of burning plastic and gas. I remember moaning, "Ouch, ouch." I then heard Audrey screaming and soon my son did too. That's when my brain started to clear, and I focused on getting out of the car. The sound of my children's screams brought me absolute joy.

I was hanging by my seatbelt because our Suburban had landed on the driver's side. I tried to undo the seatbelt but my right wrist was broken. Bones were bundled up under the skin like a rainbow. I asked Audrey if she could find her phone because I couldn't see mine. She said no, but then asked me to call OnStar. Our rearview mirror was hanging off the windshield with wires all over the place. My son started screaming, "Call 911!" After failing to get my seatbelt off, I asked Audrey if she could get out. She said yes. She used the middle console to bear weight, and broke her window with her elbow and butt. She climbed out and started screaming for help. I started to wiggle around and realized my foot was hanging in an odd direction. I could feel my khakis getting heavier as they soaked up the blood.

Audrey returned and I asked if she could get Eli out of the backseat. I could hear him wiggling around in the back, and when he made his way to the front seat I could see blood running down his face. He was crying when his big sister reached in to pull him from the wreckage.

That was the last time I would see my kids for six days.

Two men came to the passenger side of the car and I could hear one of them cussing. I told him I had a broken arm and leg but was otherwise okay. I was not in any pain and speaking clear as day. I asked if he had a knife to cut me out of my seatbelt so I wouldn't have to hang there any longer. He took off, yelling at others, and returned to bust out the back window and climb past the third row and back seat to approach me from behind. After he cut my seatbelt, I asked if he could help get me out. I tried pushing with my left leg because of my hanging foot but couldn't get very far because the steering wheel and dashboard were in my lap. I wanted to see if he could release my seat so I could scoot or lean back to go out the vehicle the way he came in. He did not feel comfortable moving me and decided to wait for help to arrive. I asked if he could call my husband so my children would have someone with them at the hospital. I could hear him on the phone saying, "Dude, it's not good." I tried to tell him I'm fine, just make sure someone is there at the hospital for the kids.

I could hear sirens in the distance. It felt like an eternity. I then heard an officer yelling, "Does anyone know where the driver of this vehicle is?" My first thought was that someone got ejected. As he approached my vehicle I heard him ask, "Is this one DOA [dead on arrival]?"

It took the firemen over an hour to secure my vehicle and cut me out. Once I was out, they cut all my clothing off and tried to strap me to a stretcher so the helicopter could transport me to the emergency room. The medic asked if I could put my leg down because it was sticking straight up in the air. I had some pain while they were getting me out of the vehicle, and feared my foot might fall off when they tried to extricate me from the wreckage. I thought my hip and butt were cramping from staying in an awkward position for so long.

When I got to the emergency room I saw my sister-in-law. She was crying. I asked if she had seen the kids and she told me they were in the same hospital, and that my ex-husband was there for Audrey. I was being poked, prodded, questioned, x-rayed, and then the doctor came in. My sister-in-law, Brenda, and former softball player Dina, who was now a DPS officer, were in the room when the doctor explained my extensive list of injuries and reported that I needed to have immediate surgery. I remember being in shock because I was sure that the arm and leg were my only injuries and I would be out of there quickly. I asked if they could call my mother in California to let her know. As I was spitting out phone numbers, they wheeled me to the operating room.

What I didn't know was that my husband Tommy had contacted a friend who lived near the crash site. When they tried to put Audrey in an ambulance along with the other driver and his ten-day-old baby, she noticed he had blood running down his face and asked to wait for the next ambulance so she could ride with her brother. A friend rode with our two children in the ambulance to the hospital. Tommy called all his family within an hour's drive. My son and a three-year-old girl who was a passenger in the truck were airlifted to Covenant Children's Hospital in Lubbock, Texas.

Audrey walked out of the emergency room barefoot and in borrowed scrubs because her clothes had been cut off at the scene and her shoes were soaked in blood. Tommy's identical twin and other family members went to Lubbock to be there for Elijah. They thought he could have internal bleeding. Tommy left the softball fields in Las Vegas in shock to try to contact my family and change his flight home.

When I woke from surgery, everything was a blur except the metal bars sticking out of my leg. I anticipated seeing Brenda, my sister-in-law, but it was my two good friends, and they were very upset. I asked where Brenda was, and they explained that she had gone to Lubbock to be with Elijah who needed stitches and staples to his head. I remembered the way he looked when he crawled over my seat, but I didn't know that he was classified as serious because of possible internal injuries from the seatbelt.

My father and stepfather were two people I saw that day who looked worried. I tried to reassure them that everything was going to be okay; bones heal. When my mother flew in from California the next day, the doctor explained to her the extent of my injuries. I had an open pilon fracture on my right ankle, which meant it was crushed. The first surgery was to clean the ankle of bone fragment and debris. They inserted an external fixator which looked like a bicycle kickstand to keep my legs the same length. Before they rolled me into surgery, the doctor told my mom that they weren't sure whether they could save my leg. They were going to try because at age thirty-two I was so young, but it just depended on how much bone loss there was. My hip needed to be plated and my arm needed pins to stabilize my wrist. I spent five days in critical care and a total of twelve days in the hospital.

After my second round of surgeries, I found out that the car who hit the truck was a drunk driver who left the scene on foot. His face and name were shown on local media, so anyone who knew who or where he was could come forward with information. His name was Cody and I resented him for taking off, leaving behind seven injured people. He ran away as Audrey screamed for help. He left behind a man who pleaded for someone to help his wife, three-year-old daughter, and newborn infant who was just ten days old. Cody hid in the dark until he finally knocked on someone's door at 3 a.m. asking to use their phone—he wanted to call for a ride home.

Cody left his car at the scene and never claimed it from the wrecking yard. All his belongings were still in it. My husband

Tommy went to take pictures of the vehicles at the wrecking yard, and saw Cody's mail and other items he left on his seat. The car still smelled of alcohol days after the wreck.

It was recommended that I go to a nursing home because I was going to be bedridden for several months. I was non-weight bearing on three out of four limbs. I needed help to sit up and learn how to use a slide board for transfers to a wheelchair. I needed to have the dressings changed on my wounds, rolled so I didn't get bedsores, bathed, given medication and fed. My mother knew that she could not physically handle all that, so she and Tommy began touring nursing homes.

Audrey and Elijah were not allowed to visit me in the hospital, so I thought moving to a facility where they could visit would be the best situation. My mom returned from the tours to notify me that I could not get into the good nursing homes because of age requirements. The homes that I could get into were not up to par for my mother, and she thought the kids would not want to go there to visit. In the end, we decided that I would come home. My father built me a ramp so I could enter my own home. I had to arrive in an ambulance because I could not use the slide board to get from my wheelchair into my SUV. We cleared the dining room and moved in a hospital bed, bedside commode, and a TV tray to hold my belongings. I was bathed a few feet away in the kitchen. I hid behind a shower curtain hanging on a portable clothes rack to do my duties. Anyone who was in the living room or playroom knew I was done when I moved the curtain and sprayed. It was so embarrassing because I had become so helpless. I had to be sponge-bathed by Audrey and my mother, wear a bib when I ate because I was not left handed, and had to eat in my bed.

My mother moved in to take on all of my duties. She carted my kids to and from school and athletic activities. My father and mother had not been under the same roof since I was an infant. Now these two ex-spouses would have to deal with each other and care for me like I was an infant. Their snide comments to one another were both entertaining and frustrating.

I started reading books and binge watching Netflix on my iPad. If I didn't feel like talking or eating that day, I rolled over to face the wall and acted like I was asleep. I would cry and try to conceal the sniffling because I really did not want to differentiate between the emotional and physical pain.

I had so many people calling, texting, emailing, Facebooking, fundraising, and stopping by to visit me that I just wanted to be alone. I wanted to try to process all that had happened without having to filter it with a smile and a happy ending. I tried to be thankful that we had all lived and were only dealing with broken bones, but anger started to build inside. I wanted the driver to know what it felt like to be broken and in constant pain. I wanted his children to draw pictures of him in a wheelchair. I thought about making a visit to that address on the envelope left in the gold Kia Optima. I wanted him to look me in the face. I wanted him to know what he walked away from that night: kids screaming, two women who were so broken that they might not be the same again, a man holding his newborn with blood running down his face, crying to his wife, who was unconscious in a ditch. I wanted Cody to get the six-figure bills that were being sent to my house right before Thanksgiving. I wanted him debating what Christmas was going to look like for his children. Honestly, I didn't mind the pain, I just didn't think it was fair that he was not injured and might not be caught because of how many wrongs he had done.

The car he was driving wasn't registered in his name. He had purchased it with cash the month before and didn't have it insured. My attorney said that he wouldn't be pursued because he didn't have enough assets and would probably file bankruptcy, and I wouldn't get anything. In my opinion, the officer did a poor job investigating the crash. In fact, it took two weeks to get a crash report, and it was filled with errors.

The first crash report was based on the driver of the Lincoln who said that a vehicle came into his lane which caused him to brake. The Kia rear-ended his passenger side which sent him into my lane where he crashed into me. When I realized people were trying to cover themselves, I called the officer to tell him there were mistakes in the report that needed correcting. The officer basically said I could reword the report, but it would be my word against his. That sent me into a downward spiral because an official report should always reflect the truth. The driver of the Kia was at fault because he was driving too close to the Lincoln. The report was amended stating that a phantom car caused the Lincoln to brake which led to the initial crash, and then the second crash. I was so infuriated that the truth wasn't recorded, and very little would be done to find the driver.

I wondered how I was going to keep up with all these bills: three medical insurances, two hospitals, our car insurance, and an attorney. Within a month I was back in the emergency room with a staph infection in my left leg from an open wound. This was my first time out of the house and not in an ambulance. I was treated twice the weekend after Thanksgiving because the infection had spread to the pins in my arm and the incision on my hip. If it had reached the bone in my arm, they would have had to cut away the bone and replace all the hardware in my body.

I should have been out Christmas shopping with my mother-in-law and sister-in-law. After Thanksgiving dinner, it was tradition for the kids to look through ads and form wish lists. We would then hit the stores all night and the next day, nap, and then hit the rest of the sales later that weekend. Now, not only could I not go shopping, I was racking up more medical bills.

That weekend I learned how to transfer from my wheelchair to my mom's car. I could now get out of the house once in a while, and my mom suggested I go with her to the grocery store. The sun was out, and I remember feeling really good about being able to help with the grocery shopping. We pulled into a handicapped spot and were contemplating how to get me into the motorized grocery cart. As my mom opened the door, a lady in a truck pulled up behind our car, rolled down her window and yelled, "I can't see your placard! Are you handicapped?"

My mother proceeded to tell her in a matter of fact way that she wasn't handicapped, but I was. The lady pulled off and parked in the handicapped spot directly in front of us. As my mother was walking into the store to get a motorized cart for me, the lady got out of her truck and said, "It looks like you can walk just fine!" My mom lost her cool. As she rode the cart back to our car, she yelled back, "I already told you! It's not me who's handicapped, it's my daughter! Oh, and you look like you can walk just fine yourself!" Here I was with my car door open, anxious to transfer to my first motorized cart but by the time I made it into the store, I was furious. I wanted to shout, "Here I am, the young handicapped lady from whom you needed proof to park in the handicapped spot. Would you like to see my scars? Would you like my trauma surgeon's phone number or diagnosis?"

What was supposed to be an exciting and liberating moment turned into my first experience feeling judged and different. My mother felt horrible because she had good intentions for my first outing, but I just wanted to return to my bed and deal with how the world was going to view me. The old me was athletic, strong, a fighter, hard worker, and funny. Now I would be seen as fragile, damaged, needy, and wrecked. Wrecked can describe what happened that night, or how I felt inside, or how my body was.

December was always a busy month for our family. First, it was my birthday, followed by the birthdays of my father, brother, and then Elijah all in the same week. But this year the excitement felt fake. I did not get to bake my son a birthday cake, throw him a party, or fill his piñata. Instead, he had a store-bought cake and we went to the local pizzeria and arcade to celebrate. I was in a wheelchair wearing a nightgown and again dealing with the public. Luckily, I was surrounded by a few friends and their kids, but I had to explain why I had bars sticking out of my arm, and answer all their questions. I sat at the table looking at the half-eaten cake while the kids were in the arcade, thinking things might never be the same. My participation in holidays, birthdays, anniversaries, and vacations would be altered, and I didn't quite know for how long.

I started doing more physical therapy at home to prepare for the strides to come. I started marching while sitting on the edge of my bed, and worked putty in my right hand in an effort to regain function. Eventually, when the hip x-rays came back looking good, I was released to begin weightbearing on my left leg. I used a walker with a platform to rest my right arm in order to get out of bed, and raised my hospital bed to the highest position so it wouldn't take as much work. I remember feeling scared that I might fall or accidentally put weight on my right foot, which was still trying to grow new bone. I worried that I just couldn't do it. On my first attempt to get out of bed, my legs shook and I had no balance or strength, and immediately fell back on the bed. I began sitting and standing on one leg several times a day and lowered the bed a little each time to give the quivering leg a real workout.

Just before Christmas I had surgery to remove hardware from my right arm. A cast was placed that went just above my elbow but it inhibited my slide board operations and using the platform on the walker. I felt like I had taken a small step backward. I was in more pain now, and my hand, fingers and arm hurt almost constantly. I started taking more pain medication which then required other medications so I could sleep through the night.

I eventually started using the walker for transfers and could finally get rid of the plastic slide board, though I had several marks from being pinched and experienced my first fall to the ground. But now I could rely on one leg to move my body from object to object. I would be able to transfer myself using the walker, which meant going to the bathroom without needing to wake someone in the middle of the night. I stumbled twice and accidentally put weight on my right foot which was still healing, but still it was progress.

Our church puts on a family event the weekend before the kids get out for Christmas break. There are hayrides to look at Christmas lights, a bonfire, hot chocolate, kettle corn, and a fabulous candlelight service. This year I arrived in a wheelchair and wore a nightgown instead of a hospital gown so I could attend. I covered my hardware with a blanket and saw many familiar faces. I wanted to shy away, but I knew they had been praying for us and providing us with so much support. I sat in the back where there was room for my wheelchair. When they stood to participate in praise and worship, I sat there wishing that I could stand too. I became emotional with every song and started to cry. I felt selfish because of my suffering, but then realized I wouldn't be in the back forever. I would stand again, be able to raise my hand, and would continue to live. Sitting in the back changed my perspective in many ways. There was hope that I would heal not in my time, but in God's time. I needed to be patient and focus on the process.

Christmas was a time we usually spent with extended family. We either took a trip to California to be with my family, or went just down the road to be with Tommy's family. That Christmas, I did not do any shopping. I tried shopping online but became very irritated with the process, so Tommy and my mom did the shopping. The kids put the tree up and tried to decorate the house.

I saw the first snow from my bed through the dining room window, and the kids brought me icicles from the backyard. I thought about the last time we had taken our family picture in the backyard in the snow. We built a snowman and tried to get the two dogs in the picture as well. I took many trips back and forth to the camera on the tripod because either one dog was looking and the other wasn't, or Elijah was making a silly face.

As if things weren't hard enough that winter, our black lab Chico passed away. He suffered for a while, but I couldn't bear to look at him like that anymore. Tommy took Chico to the vet to be put down. I was upset not only because we lost a family member of nine years, but that I couldn't be there to hold Chico when he died. Emotions ran high for the next few days for our entire family. I started feeling guilty and anxious, and started curling up in the bed facing the wall to cry myself to sleep. As the year came to a close, I felt angry, full of pain and fear, and bent on revenge. Our family was emotionally drained by all of the changes we were working so hard to get used to.

When the new year began, I wanted only a better year than the previous one. January was a month of steadfast. I anxiously waited for restrictions to be removed so I could gain more liberties. Standing up and sitting transitioned into using one leg and a walker to move around a few steps. I was able to get into the kids' bathroom and sit on a bench and shower with a plastic bag on my cast. I tried to shower with one arm using the removable shower head. This was one of the first accomplishments that made me feel like things were finally starting to normalize.

I started writing in a journal led by devotionals that were brought to me from the prayer team at church. My writings were so different from what I typed on my phone in a locked diary app.

I loosened my obsessive internet search for the driver that had peaked during December. My need for the driver to experience my pain faded, but I still yearned for him to know the repercussions of his decision to get behind the wheel intoxicated. During the waiting periods between x-ray results and doctor appointments, I really looked forward to returning to my classroom. I started looking at lesson plans for after spring break.

I was looking forward to February so I could start traditional physical therapy. When I entered the physical therapy office with my walker, I was greeted with a warm welcome. I had just been through ACL reconstruction on my left knee. I knew that it was going to be a long, hard road to recovery but I was excited to move forward. Three times a week I spent almost two and a half hours in that office for physical therapy on my hip, wrist and ankle. I entered the first day using a walker with support for my right arm. It wasn't long before I graduated to a quad cane and then a traditional cane. My wrist and fingers were the most painful those first couple of weeks but progressed very quickly. My hip had very limited range of motion but the leg was strong. My right leg was very weak and the ankle was in constant pain. The scars were pulled on, and my range of motion was pushed to the point where I thought I was going to pass out. After each session I left a full body imprint of sweat on the table. I wondered how long it was going to be like this.

When I returned to my doctor with improvements, he released me to start driving again. This was nerve-wracking and liberating at the same time. I drove a short distance from the ballfields to Chick-fil-A and realized that this was going to be a process. I could hardly hold my foot on the brake because of pain. I knew that I was close, but needed more time to heal. Once I felt confident that I was capable of driving safely, my mom went home.

Tommy wanted me to attend his athletic banquet and visit with people I hadn't seen in about six months. I wanted to buy a new blouse to wear with a long skirt to cover the scars on my ankle and left leg. An associate opened a dressing room and said she would be back to see if I needed anything. I hobbled in with my cane and started to try on blouses but once I looked in the mirror and saw myself, I broke down and cried. I saw scars everywhere. I would have to cover up from head to toe so the wreck wouldn't be the only conversation that night. I began crying uncontrollably and couldn't stop. I texted my mom from the dressing room to try to work up the courage to leave with my blotchy red face and runny nose. I left the clothes in the dressing room and hung my head and stared at the ground as I made my way toward the store exit. As I passed by the register, the associate asked if I was okay. The only thing I could get out was, "It's just too soon to be doing this." I was ashamed of how I looked. I knew my scars would never go away, a lifelong reminder of what I had been through. I wasn't sure if I was ready to face these hidden feelings without my mother.

I cannot express how much my mom sacrificed to be here for my family and me. She already had roundtrip tickets to come visit us, and was going to take Audrey to San Antonio for her first concern to see Selena Gomez, her favorite singer. Mom had to reschedule her roundtrip flights to arrive sooner to help pick up the pieces of our wrecked family.

Three weeks after the wreck, Mom was supposed to go to Costa Rica with my aunt, but she canceled and gave her prepaid trip to my aunt's friend.

Mom was away from her own bed, dogs, husband and son for four months, and forced to live with her ex-husband so she could tend to me and my family. She dealt with my emotional and physical pain. She guided us through paying bills and processing insurance notifications. Without my mom, my family's progress would have been much slower. I would have been stuck in a nursing home, and likely wouldn't have done as well. Her sacrifices will never be forgotten.

I continued physical therapy until June. The kids were out of school, and I felt confident driving and walking short distances with a cane. We decided to stay in California with Mom for a month. I joined a gym to keep up my physical therapy exercises and used her pool every day to stretch and exercise. I made a trip to Disneyland in a wheelchair and was limited to certain rides that I was confident I could transfer onto. I knew that being pushed around in a wheelchair was going to be difficult, but I didn't expect it to give rise to all the emotions I thought I had buried. I started to get angry again.

I began having nightmares about meeting the driver through a mutual friend or bumping into each other in a public place. My biggest fear was how I might react when we met face-to-face. Would I seek vengeance? Would I freeze? Would I act like nothing had happened, try to gain his trust, and then tell him who I was? So many scenarios entered my dreams. The worst dream I had was one where I was walking with my two children and a man followed us to our front door. When I turned to defend myself, all I had was my cane. I poked it at the man but it didn't help. I remember feeling so helpless because I could not run from the situation, nor could I defend myself and my children.

These fears returned the day I took a trip to the beach, a trip I thought would rejuvenate my peace and stillness. The beach is a place where I used to go to cleanse my soul. I would think about how large the ocean is and how small I am, and it never failed to put into perspective how little my worries really are in the grand scheme of things. I let the waves take me as they willed, and I learned to let go and ride the waves.

But instead of filling me with peace, this trip filled me with fear and anxiety. I had a hard time walking with a cane on the sand. My balance was challenged by the pounding waves and I fell. I decided to just go with it and get into the water. I swam for about thirty minutes but when I wanted to get out of the water, things took a turn for the worse. With my back to the waves and the water below my waist, I struggled to get out. So I got down on my belly to get as close to the beach as I could and then tried to stand, but was repeatedly knocked down by waves. My friend and Audrey saw me struggling and brought my cane. I was covered in sand from head to toe, and completely embarrassed. I didn't swim the rest of the day. I sat in my beach chair watching Audrey learn to boogieboard and Elijah build sandcastles. When Elijah ran toward the water to jump over the little waves, I feared I wouldn't be able to reach him fast enough if something were to happen. I felt as helpless as I did in my dream. My physical limitations were taking a toll on my confidence and self-worth.

After our trip to California, I returned home for more x-rays to see if healing was taking place. While the doctor was impressed with my improvement, he wouldn't release me back to work. I put in for a leave of absence and wouldn't return to work that schoolyear. I asked to start water therapy because being in my mother's pool every day seemed to be easier and less painful. I joined YMCA because they had water aerobics and a water arthritis class three times a week. I spent hours every week in the water working on balance and range of motion for my hip and ankle.

Just before my one-year checkup, I was frustrated because I had come a long way but was not even close to where I wanted to be. This would be the last exam with my trauma surgeon. They would not continue regular x-rays, which led me to believe that all the healing was done. I was still in constant pain and very limited. I tried pushing a cart in the grocery store instead of a walking device, but this caused swelling and miserable pain the rest of the day. I had a hard time coping with the new me.

Recently I started feeling pain while working out in the water, which was new. I pushed through the pain until I was on a trip with Tommy and his team. I could feel grinding and locking in the ankle, and couldn't put any pressure on it. I was in tears because I knew something was wrong. I went to an urgent care clinic for x-rays, thinking a screw was out of place. But the x-ray showed a nonunion of bone — gaps that never healed. I called home to my surgeon only to discover that he was no longer in my area. I returned home in a tremendous amount of pain and no doctor.

I had to jump through insurance hoops to get a referral to a new orthopedic surgeon. He sent me for a CT scan, and two weeks later I was told that my hardware was out of place and I had several sites of nonunion. I was referred to a foot and ankle specialist.

At this point I was in so much pain I begged for an amputation, but my new surgeon was the first doctor who gave me hope. We planned for removal of the hardware and a bone graft to fill in the nonunion sites, and if the ankle joint was not stable, new hardware would be added. He took bone marrow from the center of my femur and used donor bone to fill in the ankle. This procedure sent me back to a nonweight-bearing status to give the bone time to heal.

The surgeon felt we could address the damage to the joint after I recovered from surgery, which would take about a year. I walked out of his office feeling hopeful that I might one day be able to walk normally again. Hopefully, after my ankle was fixed I could then get the needed hip replacement. I knew I had a long recovery road ahead. My faith in healing had many ups and downs, but now I felt hope that I might return to my old self.

My emotional relationship with Cody, the driver, has evolved. I still keep up with him through social media now and then. I long for the chance to be able to impact his life. I want him to know that his actions changed my life forever, along with those who surround me. Even with a possibility of healing, there has been a tear in my trust for law enforcement, lawyers, and insurance.

I have a wonderful support system at home, in California, and online. Without a safe place to vent, I would've given up. Knowing that there are people out there feeling the same way, some who are in worse situations, helps me to stay strong and use my voice.

I talk to many young adults and teens about the importance of making good decisions and how quickly life can change. On the night of the wreck, things could have been completely avoided if the driver had called for a ride after drinking instead of causing a head-on collision.

I am grateful I was able to survive to witness to those around me. I believe we had perfectly bad timing that night. If we had been half a second off, our wreck would have been fatal. The newborn in the truck who collided with us was due the night of the wreck. If the mother had still been pregnant, he would not have survived. I am thankful for what we still have, although it is hard to not look back on what I had. Our planned vacations, school trips, athletic seasons, church and career activities have changed drastically because of that night. I honestly hope that one day I can look back and feel confident that sharing my story helps someone change for the better. I want those who feel they are not going to make it, or want to quit, to realize that it will get better. The scars I see every day in the mirror will fade but never go away. They will always serve as a reminder of where I've been — and how strong I can be.

\*

AMANDA RIDDELL
Amanda was 26 when she and her three
children were hit by a drunk driver in 2003

On November 10, 2003, I was trying to decide whether to take my daughter to her dance lesson. I really didn't feel like bundling up the children as it was starting to get late and it was almost half an hour drive to Cranbrook. I remember thinking to myself, "I should just stay home but I can't. She missed last week. I need to take her," and off we went. As I drove toward Cranbrook from Kimberley, almost ten minutes out of town, I saw a car coming from my left at a side junction. It was speeding, and I knew we were going to collide. He ran the stop sign. I braced and whipped my arm across my son's chest. His feet braced against the dashboard. The music stopped. There was no noise, no sound. I could feel my body flinging as the car hit us almost head-on.

No sound. I remember this clearly—how can there be no sound but I can see you? Then I heard my oldest son screaming his sister's name. I spun around to check on them. My daughter was screaming loudly—so loudly. Off in the distance I could hear sirens. Then I saw the man who hit us—he was trying to get away. Another truck went after him and the driver held him. That was the last thing I remember before the firetrucks blocked my view that dark night.

\*

JEWEL ROSE
Jewel was 39 when she and her family
were hit by a drunk driver in 2012

I was relieved to be able to get away for a weekend. I had just completed training in the collection of data on interventions, and two particular coworkers obviously had some very negative preconceived notions about that! My stress level was quite high, but I had landed by dream job and I was learning more about the nuances of at-risk youth when my family and I decided to go camping. The weekend was so wonderful! We rode motorcycles, sat by the campfire, and I was able to get much needed sleep. It was really interesting that the kids tried to talk us into getting a new trailer. I told them how I loved the trailer and how their dad had updated the interior and how perfect it was. I was not in the market for a new trailer or truck. The kids even loaded wood without complaining! My husband turned off the propane tanks just before we pulled out of the camping spot. I had no idea how important that would be in only a few moments.

We had traveled a few miles down the highway when my husband reminded me to put on my seatbelt. I was a little irritated that he was bugging me to put it on, but I reluctantly clicked it together. Just as I settled in, I looked up and saw a truck heading into our lane as we were turning the corner. We often travel so I was expecting the truck to correct. But it didn't. I could see it heading straight for us. I remember looking up toward the sky and asking, "God, is today the day I am going to see you?" A truck was heading straight for us. My husband tried to avoid the truck by driving off the highway and straight to a cliff. So I knew today was the day. I felt eternity. It is real. Death is so final.

At the last minute, the truck moved a few inches to the left and drove down the side of our truck. I saw it heading for my husband and son, and knew they would not survive. I just kept looking ahead so I wouldn't have to see my husband and son die, and just waited for us to roll over. I knew that most head-on collisions with trucks pulling trailers resulted in rollover accidents. Yet we didn't roll — we just kept skidding across the highway. We didn't roll, nor did we hit any other car when four vehicles crossed both lanes of the highway.

After each vehicle came to a stop, my kids ran to the driver's truck. It was on fire. Someone came with a fire extinguisher and put out the flames. My sons peeled away the sheet metal from the driver's truck. They thought he was dead. I tried to run to my sons, but the trailer was blocking the entire highway and in my way. I could see through the trailer and I began looking for my dog, Chukar. He was not in his kennel. I expected to see a mangled mess and a smashed dog. I called for him and he rounded the corner and jumped into my arms. People were asking if I was okay, and Chukar barked at them. He normally would never do that, but he was scared. I put him in the cab of our truck since his kennel was obliterated. He had no safe place to go other than our cab.

I tried to find the driver. "Where is the driver?" I asked. A bystander from one of the cars said, "Follow me." I was led me to a travel trailer where the driver was hiding on the floor. I could see blood on the pony wall. The bystander said to the driver "Your go'en." I was too confused to realize that the driver had prior drunk driving charges. I could see he wasn't wearing shoes as he then tried to walk up a hill. Traffic was backed up for miles. This was May in northern Idaho; the weather was still very cold, and it wasn't safe to walk anywhere without shoes. I began to talk softly to the driver, and told him that he needed help. His head and arm were bleeding, and broken glass was everywhere. I coaxed him back to his truck. That is when I saw the beer can. With every fiber in my body, I fought to control my anger and the strong urge to pummel this guy. I knew I could kick his drunken body to the next century, but I also knew that if I did that, any good that my family could get out of this mess would be gone. I had to remain calm.

The aid car finally came to take him to the hospital. I walked around the trailer and my stomach hurt really bad. I thought, "My sons can't see me hurt. If I just bend over a little bit, they won't see me hurt and it will be okay." The next thing I knew, a firefighter was covering my shoulders with a blanket and giving me water. My son told them about the sulfur smell coming from the trailer, and about my shock. A few minutes later I was in the ambulance headed to the hospital. That was when I lost consciousness.

\*

MICHAEL SMITH
Michael's 39-year-old brother Patrick
was killed by an impaired driver in 2007

Patrick was an engaging, humorous, outgoing personality who loved his son, Dakota, more than anything. I always knew my brother was a giving person, but I didn't understand many others also felt the same way until his wake. More than three hundred people lined up on a cold December night to pay their respects to my brother.

Patrick's caring personality kept him busy outside his job at Gerber Scientific. He had a hectic schedule picking Dakota up from his mother's house and later dropping him off, but somehow managed to keep everything in order even though he didn't have nearly enough time to himself.

Patrick was driving to work on Route 74 from Mansfield, Connecticut. He was at an intersection when an impaired diabetic driving a Dodge Dakota sped through a red light and crashed into the side of Patrick's Saturn sedan. The force from the impact was so severe it sent Patrick's car flying diagonally across the street, crushing his driver's seat into the passenger seat. Patrick suffered massive internal injuries but didn't die instantly. Eyewitnesses said he was breathing for several minutes before the medics arrived.

My day started at 7 a.m. with that phone call from my father. Patrick's car was crushed by an impaired, self-medicating diabetic. Although he was diagnosed with diabetes fifteen years prior, he reportedly never checked his glucose level before driving. In a hypoglycemic state, he blacked out, his car ran the red stoplight, and struck Patrick's car as he traveled through the intersection. In a stupor, the impaired driver then backed up and drove away, causing a second crash.

\*

REBECCA TIMMONS
Rebecca was 46 when she was
hit by a drunk driver in 2015

On December 9, 2015, I was driving home after hanging out with my girlfriends. I was hit by a drunk driver who was twice the legal limit and admitted to being high. He ran through a red light striking my car on my driver's side. I was airlifted to the trauma hospital. I was in a coma for two and a half weeks. My bladder, spleen and diaphragm ruptured, I was in respiratory failure, had three fractured ribs, a skull fracture, broken wrist, lacerated liver and my pelvis was fractured in four places. I remained in the hospital for a month. I had a chest tube, catheter and drain for my bladder. My bladder was removed and replaced with a balloon, my spleen was removed and my diaphragm was put back together. After I was discharged from the hospital, I was unable to stand or walk for another four months. The catheter and drain remained in for another two months and I have had several kidney infections due to the trauma. I also now suffer from PTSD and have been unable to return to work.

\*

LINDSAY WELDON
Lindsay was 21 when she was
hit by a drunk driver in 2012

I was hit by a drunk driver at 3 a.m. on November 16, 2012, while delivering the morning newspaper. I was slowing down to make a left turn into a parking lot when I saw headlights coming out of a commercial driveway to my right. I thought the car would stop and yield to the right of way. Instead, the white 2009 Honda Civic came flying out and hit the front passenger side of my car. The impact sent me across the other lane, onto a sidewalk, and into a planter against a brick wall. I had never been in a car crash before, so I got out of the car and called 911. The other driver got out of his car as well. I couldn't tell the officer on the phone where I was. All I knew was that I was on the sidewalk in front of Round Table Pizza in Los Osos. After getting off the phone with 911, I called my mom. I told her what happened, where I was, and that the police were on their way. The paramedics, police, and fire department all showed up just moments before my mom. I was rushed to a nearby hospital. I remember getting x-rays and then a CT scan of my neck and head. Four hours later I was sent home. I remember my mom waking me to take pain pills every four hours to stay ahead of the pain.

My best friend's bachelorette party was that night, and I couldn't go. Nor did I look pretty for her wedding two days later. I was in constant pain from something that wasn't my fault.

*

RACHAEL WILLIAMS
Rachael was 25 when her 30-year-old husband
Matthew was killed by a drunk driver in 2012

On May 10, 2012, my husband Matthew was walking home from work when he was hit by a drunk driver. He had lost his license in late 2011, and our vehicle was broken down. I spoke to Matthew at 10 p.m. He said someone had offered him a ride and he would be home shortly.

I woke up at 3 a.m. and realized Matthew still wasn't home. I began calling him and trying to figure out where he was. At 7 a.m., my daughter woke up and then I heard a knock on the door. Two detectives in black unmarked cars had come. They asked who I was and if Matthew lived there. I replied that I was Matthew's wife and this was his daughter. We went into the kitchen and the detectives began asking questions about Matthew. I was thinking he got into trouble and I needed to bail him from jail. They then told me that he had been involved in an accident at 3 a.m. just down the street. When I asked if Matthew was okay, they informed me that he had been killed.

The detectives asked me to come identify Matthew, but I couldn't do it. My family was called and my mom made the positive identification. They gave us all the information and said the driver had run from the scene after driving his vehicle into a culvert, but witnesses caught him. He asked to use someone's phone. When the witness asked the driver what he had hit, his response was, "I don't know. But whatever it was, I hit it good," and walked away from the accident. At about 5:30 a.m., they found the driver under a vehicle. He tried saying they had the wrong guy, but witnesses identified him and he was arrested.

*

SHELLY WOODWARD<br>
Shelly was 30 when her 16-month old son was injured in a<br>
drunk driving crash caused by Shelly's former husband in 1996

How many of us think "That will never happen to me?" I was one of those. It was May 1996, Memorial Day weekend, and my two older daughters had gone to stay with my ex-husband. I had attended a party and got home about 9 p.m. My then husband had left a note saying he had taken our sixteen-month-old son to his mom's so he could go to a friend's party. I decided to nap and then woke up. Realizing that it was late and my husband and our son should be home by now, I called his mom who said that he had already picked up our son. He should have been home, as we didn't live far. I asked if he had been drinking and his mom said yes, and started to cry. She had put my child in the car seat with a drunk.

I had no time to think, I had to find them. I called a friend who worked for the 911 dispatch. I asked her if there had been a wreck, and she responded there had. I ran to the neighbors to ask them to drive me down the road. Five miles down the road, there was my brand new Jeep flipped on its top. I knew my child was inside, but didn't know if he was dead or alive.

Our son had been born twelve weeks early, and had fought for his life. Now here he was in a crash out of his control. I ran through the crowd, saw the ambulance and heard my child screaming. I rode in the ambulance with my son, and told everyone that my husband was drunk. I didn't know they knew.

An MRI showed that my son had a closed skull fracture. He had flown out of his car seat, hit the dash, and was found in the back of the Jeep.

I divorced my husband and started a new life. I became a speaker for MADD, and a fighter for tougher DUI laws. Watching my ex-husband, a five-time offender, walk away with a hand slap was too much for me. He could have killed our son. I wanted to fight for justice.

I am lucky my son lived. He survived and is now attending college to become a veterinarian, but the damage done by an alcoholic father has created many years of mental anguish. Anguish that I hope fades with time.

*

A great soul never dies. It brings
us together again and again.

MAYA ANGELOU

*

# CHAPTER TWO

# FACING THE AFTERMATH

Somehow, even in the worst of times, the tiniest fragments of good survive. - MELINA MARCHETTA

Following any sort of trauma, we often wonder how we're going to weather the emotional and physical aftermath. Some have no recollection of the crash while others remember every terrifying detail. When the adrenaline wears off, we're left to face a future we didn't expect. How did you survive the initial aftermath?

\*

JESSICA WEYER BENTLEY
Jessica was 5 when her 24-year-old father
Robert was killed by a drunk driver in 1979

I was very young, only five years old. I blocked most of it out as part of the posttraumatic stress disorder I suffered. I have only certain memories from those early years about what happened.

\*

SHANNON BOOS
Shannon was 20 when her 21-year-old brother
Kevin was killed by a drunk driver in 2015

I like the wording of this question because a lot of people have asked me how I lived in the first few months. I didn't live. I was surviving. Every single day was making sure I was breathing, and that I still had blood pumping through my body. It sure didn't feel like I was alive, but I guess I was.

I spent two years at Florida State University with Kevin, and had earned my associate's degree. I worked really hard and was accepted into the elementary education program at the University of Florida in Gainesville, the best program in the state.

Before Kevin was killed, I was an atypical twenty-year-old college girl. All I did was workout, go to school, study, work out some more, and was always productive in some way. I would like to go out with my friends sometimes too, but I wasn't one to really sit still, especially when there were things to do. I had just started classes and was at the top of my game, on top of the world, and so happy at my new school.

The night Kevin was killed, every single thing about me changed. I did nothing. And I am not exaggerating when I use the word "nothing."

My family's dog Nala was living with me in my apartment, and to this day I believe she is one of the only reasons I'm still alive. She needed me get out of bed to walk her, feed her, etc. But that was the only time I would really get up. I would typically wake up hungover, would probably vomit a couple of times, and I would crawl right back into bed. I'd get up to walk Nala whenever she let me know she needed to go outside, but besides that, I would hide under my covers with the lights off. Then 7 p.m. would hit and I saw this as an acceptable time to start drinking. That is when I would start my one or two bottles of wine, and drink until I couldn't see straight.

I can remember back in 2013, when I was a freshman in college and Kevin had his own cool apartment with a few friends and they threw parties all the time. I would attend, of course, and bring friends, and it was always a night to remember. However, there was one night when I drank way too much trying to cover up some heartbreak that I was going through. I remember vomiting in Kevin's bathroom, bawling my eyes out, and screaming for him. He came running, and didn't leave my side the whole night, even while I was throwing up and inconsolable. Even though his friends had all left to go to a club, he stayed with me. He was there.

Two years later I found myself in the bathroom, drunk beyond belief, vomiting, and hysterically crying. But this time, I would lay on the cold tile floor alone, and no matter how many times I would scream his name, he wouldn't come. And every single time the roaring silence would rip a bigger hole into my chest.

I didn't live after he was killed. But I did survive. And to this day, I truly cannot tell you how.

*

TIFFANY COLSON<br>Tiffany was 30 when she was<br>hit by a drunk driver in 2011

I do remember the crash. I was alert the whole time. Luckily, the fire department was less than a mile away so they got there very quickly. The crash happened about 8:05 p.m. and I was at the hospital at 9:10. I believe that the reason I was so alert and felt no pain was from the adrenaline rush of it all.

*

WENDY DAVIDSON<br>Wendy was 47 when her 28-year-old son<br>Chuck was killed by a drunk driver in 2016

My son did not survive the crash even though he was wearing his seatbelt. According to police, he was killed instantly. His death certificate reads "multiple blunt force trauma." I really can't comprehend what that means exactly. I know that when my kids

59

rode their bicycles when they were younger, I always made them wear a helmet so they didn't damage their brain if they fell, but somehow I can't comprehend how it killed my son. It's simply something I can't wrap my head around.

We never saw my son after his crash. I really don't like calling it an accident, as it was completely avoidable. I have no idea as to the extent of his injuries. It terrifies me knowing that I will see the damage to my son's car, or that I'm going to see violently mangled photos of him in court. I'm haunted by those images almost daily. I play out the crash in my mind and try to visualize what my son would have seen. It's a horrible thought, but for some reason those images just won't go away, it's pure torment. I want to imagine him looking as if he were sleeping in his car the night he died. No blood, no violence — just sleeping. I don't know how I'm going to make it through the trial.

*

BILL DOWNS
Bill's 21-year-old son Brad, 19-year-old daughter-in-law
Samantha, and 24-year-old family friend Chris
were killed by a drunk/drugged driver in 2007

Although my three kids died in the crash, the emergency personnel were there very quickly thanks to an off-duty fireman who witnessed the crash. I remember coming up on the roadblock just east of the crash and seeing all the emergency vehicles and flashing lights. They lit up the night sky and I had never seen so many emergency vehicles in my life. There was no way for me to know it was my kids laying there on the ground with sheets over them after the emergency crew got them out of the mangled vehicle. After I had learned that it was my kids in this crash, surviving was an unpleasant thought. How could I survive the senseless loss of my three kids? Though I turned my back on God the first four years after the kids' death, God never gave up on me. This love from God and my wife is how I survived, and I now lean on God and my wife more than ever.

\*

JULIE DOWNS
Julie's 21-year-old son Brad, 19-year-old daughter-in-law
Samantha, and 24-year-old family friend Chris
were killed by a drunk/drugged driver in 2007

Bill and I left the hospital the morning after the crash knowing that our three kids were dead because of a drunk driver. It was so hard to process this. We drove home in silence. I was lost deep within myself. I felt dead. The person I had been died with my kids. It wasn't a gradual death, it happened immediately. I did not know how to live without my son. I didn't want to live without him. I had loved him even before they placed him in my arms the day he was born. Continuing to live just seemed impossible. I still had my handicapped daughter and Bill to care for, but I wanted my son. I was consumed with what I had lost.

There were five days between the crash and the funeral, and I functioned on autopilot. I went through the motions because things had to be done. All three of the kids were living with us at the time of the crash. The house was so quiet and I didn't know what to do with the silence. I spent my time putting their lives in a box. I had to separate Samantha's things from Brad's, but I felt that Samantha's family and Chris' mom would find comfort in their belongings. It was all that was left of them besides memories. Touching their things, smelling them and holding them to my heart made me feel closer to them but yet so far away. Each item was stained with my tears as I packed up what was left of their lives. Brad's things stayed where they were. I was not able or ready to pack them away. I wanted to see him so badly but the funeral home kept putting me off. They kept saying that he wasn't ready yet.

I talked with Samantha's mom and we agreed that Brad and Samantha would be buried side by side. Chris' mom decided to have him cremated. Bill asked if she would allow us to have some of his ashes to be with Brad and Samantha; she said yes. We made arrangements to go see Chris and say our goodbyes. It wasn't easy looking at the still body of a young man who had won our hearts and became part of our family. We loved him as if he were our son.

The crash made front page news, so the phone rang off the hook as family and friends found out what happened. I did my best to comfort them. The news was a shock to everyone, and it seemed so unreal. I was in a daze. The reality hadn't yet settled in, and I felt numb. I knew the kids were dead but in my mind, I kept thinking that any moment they would come walking through the door. I just wanted to wake up from the nightmare. But the thing was, how could I wake up when I couldn't even sleep? At night I would sit outside on my front porch so I wouldn't disturb Bill while he tried to get some rest. I would cry and stare into the darkness, asking "Why?" I wouldn't be out there for long before one of my sisters, Susan or Sandy, would walk over and sit with me. I believe that each night they took turns so I wouldn't be alone. We would sit in silence, each of us lost in our own thoughts and I lost in my pain. When I had the urge to talk, they would listen and we would cry together. I was so thankful to have them living close by.

Bill was trying hard to be strong for me, but I could see the pain in his eyes. I tried not to add my pain to his, so I leaned heavily on my sisters who were my lifeline. Their presence was comforting and they helped me keep my thoughts straight. My brain was not functioning right. The pain was so intense that I was having one panic attack after another. Minutes turned into hours, hours into days, and yet my world, my life, had stopped in time.

After the funeral when family and friends went home, the food stopped coming, the phone calls ceased, and Bill went back to work. The shock wore off and the pain consumed my very being. I felt as if my baby, my child, my son had been ripped from my body. The emotional pain was so intense that it became a physical pain. I was so exhausted from not being able to sleep at night that as soon as Bill would leave for work I would crawl into bed and curl into the fetal position, hug Brad's pillow, and sleep. Sleep was the only time I found any comfort. When I was asleep I wasn't thinking, so I slept as often as I could.

I did the basic things I had to do to care for Cindy and Bill, but other than that I could not function. I cared about nothing. I tried to engage in life, but the panic attacks I was having left me lifeless and disoriented, so I isolated myself in my home until my sisters stepped in and stopped me from willing myself to die. They decided that since I had quit work and was home all day, I could start cooking dinner and have it ready for when my sisters and my other family who lived close by got home from work. Not knowing how to say no, I agreed. So that is what I did. Five days a week, I spent the day planning dinner, cooking and crying in between. There would be anywhere from five to twelve people over each night. I didn't realize it until later, but my sisters giving me a purpose in life gave me a reason to live. Food became my comfort. In a sense, it was my drug of choice.

\*

MICHAEL GERSHE
Michael was 8-weeks-old when his 28-year-old
mother Barbara was killed by a drunk driver in 1970

Luckily, I do not remember the crash since I was only four weeks old. I didn't find out that I was in the crash that killed my mother until I was a kid. I don't think I had the mental capacity to fully understand the significance of it because I was too busy just being a kid. I knew my mother was deceased and that I had almost died, but what kid can really process that? My brother was three at the time of the crash and doesn't remember it since he was sleeping, and my father does not recall seeing the car lights of the drunk driver who hit us.

According to the police report, the first officer arrived on the scene at 11:06 p.m. The fire department arrived at 11:16 p.m., and the ambulance at 11:20 p.m. My father, brother, mother and myself were all taken to the hospital to be treated for our injuries

While I don't have any recollection of the crash, the mental aspect of surviving the crash started to take its toll in college when I started to think about my own mortality and existence of being alive. It took eighteen years for me to really start comprehending the magnitude of the crash that killed my mother and almost myself. Swimming helped me survive the emotions, as I would swim "angrily" in practice and in meets. That was the best outlet for me at that time. Somehow I survived that car crash and now, for the first time, I was trying to understand why. I'm always surviving the aftermath though, that never goes away.

*

ANNETTE HANKS
Annette was 39 when she and her husband and their
13-month-old granddaughter were hit by a drunk driver in 2013

We believe that God put a police officer across the street at a business for a burglary report less than a minute before the crash. He was at our van seconds after impact. I remember everything about the impact. The sounds echo through my head. The scariest thing I remember is holding my granddaughter's head steady and thinking that she was dead the whole time. That was terrifying.

*

### RENE LEDFORD
Rene's 25-year-old son Justin Colt
was killed by a drunk driver in 2015

Justin was killed instantly. He and his friend were thrown backward onto the street and ditch. His friend does not remember anything of the crash.

*

### LINDA PAULSON
Linda was 40 when her husband and their two
young sons were killed by a drunk driver in 2003

My husband and two young sons were killed in the crash. I don't remember anything about the crash.

*

### NICOLE RAMOS
Nicole was 32 when she and her two
children were hit by a drunk driver in 2013

I saw a set of headlights come over the horizon of a hill as I accelerated to the speed limit of 75. I barely noticed another car tailgating the truck coming in my direction before I saw the car rear-end the truck on the passenger side bumper. The impact sent the truck into a spin toward my lane. I saw the blinding headlights and then a deafening sound before everything went black.

After our vehicle stopped rolling and the dust settled, I started to moan. I then heard the kids screaming, and was relieved we had all survived. I was hanging from my seatbelt because our car landed on the driver's side. I tried to unfasten my seatbelt but then noticed that my right arm was broken. I was told later that the two arm bones had been shoved over my wrist, which looked like a ball of bones in the wrist area. I tried again to unfasten my seatbelt with a mangled wrist but realized it was still locked.

I asked my thirteen-year-old daughter if she could get out of the vehicle, and she could. She had no visible signs of injury but was still in shock. She had to break out the passenger window with her elbow, climb out and then slide down the roof into the ditch we had landed in. She got out and flagged oncoming traffic so someone could call 911. When Audrey returned to our vehicle, I asked if she could get her three-year-old brother out. For her to reach him, he had to slip from his booster seat and his seatbelt, and climb over the middle console so she could lift him through the passenger window. That was when I realized that my right foot was dangling in the wrong direction. I could feel my khakis getting heavier as it soaked up blood. Bystanders called my husband and emergency services, and tried to free me from the seatbelt.

When the first officer arrived on scene, he asked if everyone in our vehicle was alive, and whether anyone knew where the driver of the other car was. As I was trapped in our Suburban, I immediately thought that someone in the truck was ejected. It seemed like forever before the fire crew arrived and started to cut me out. I am not sure how we survived a head-on collision with an impact of over 100 mph.

*

AMANDA RIDDELL
Amanda was 26 when she and her three
children were hit by a drunk driver in 2003

I had three young children in the car: my eight-year-old son, my three-year-old daughter, and my six-month-old son. It felt like time stopped and help wasn't fast enough. Although I had chest pain, that was the least of my fears. I was more worried about the impact my daughter had received. She was in a five-point car seat and was rushed to the hospital because of seatbelt injuries. Her wee body was bruised from head to toe, every point where the seatbelt touched her was bruised. I remember seeing the flashing lights as they drove off with my only daughter. My youngest boy was still asleep, and my other son seemed okay.

The one thing that stuck out in my mind, even to this day, is how the music was playing on the radio and all of a sudden it was silent. I was in deep shock, and having chest pain. I was checked out at the hospital and finally sent home. I laid in my bed and couldn't move, the pain was out of this world. Tears rolled down my cheeks and I called 911 again. A doctor in a big city found that I had two fractured vertebrae with a bulging disk touching my nerves.

Things changed fast for me that night. I was going to be an R.N., and I was almost there. Now I live in daily pain, and still undergo procedures to help me cope. My life did a full one-eighty in five and a half seconds. It will forever be an unforgettable moment in time.

*

MICHAEL SMITH
Michael's 39-year-old brother Patrick
was killed by an impaired driver in 2007

I went into anger mode, searching nonstop for days to find similar incidents and for ways to have the other driver punished. I stayed in anger mode for a very long time.

*

LINDSAY WELDON
Lindsay was 21 when she was
hit by a drunk driver in 2012

I survived the initial aftermath with a lot of help from my mom and grandpa. My mom took care of all the insurance stuff, and kept me ahead of the pain with my pain pills. At the time of the crash, I was driving my brother's car. My grandpa retired from the company who insured my brother's car, so he helped my mom understand the insurance language and told us what they could do from their standpoint. He also got us in touch with a couple of lawyers who helped us figure out what to do about the mounting medical bills.

I was the only one injured in my crash. It took probably about fifteen to twenty minutes for help to arrive, but it felt longer than that. My mom, who lives about ten minutes away from the crash site, woke my little sister up, hopped in the car, and drove to the scene, almost beating the emergency crews.

I remember the crash very clearly. What I remember the most about it was the sound of the cars crunching, and the pain that came quickly. I remember being very cold and shivering. A medic told me that my body was in shock and they would give me a blanket in the ambulance.

*

RACHAEL WILLIAMS
Rachael was 25 when her 30-year-old husband
Matthew was killed by a drunk driver in 2012

I was not at the scene when the crash occurred at 2:30 a.m. Matthew was killed but the other driver was unharmed. I was six months pregnant and had a two-year-old daughter. I'll always remember the two detectives coming to my home asking questions, and how our lives were changed forever.

\*

SHELLY WOODWARD
Shelly was 30 when her 16-month old son was injured in a
drunk driving crash caused by Shelly's former husband in 1996

My child was the only one truly injured. My former husband suffered only bruising. I remember the smell and the sight as I walked up to the crash. I will never forget hearing my child's cries in the ambulance, or the anger that overcame me for all that my baby had to go through because of his father's negligence. I remember my sister, who just found out she was pregnant, coming to stay with me at the hospital, and the sound of the heart monitor all night.

\*

Drinking and driving: there are stupider
things, but it's a very short list.

UNKNOWN

*

# CHAPTER THREE

# COPING WITH INJURIES

For me, writing is a kind of coping mechanism.
-Chuck Palahniuk

Every two minutes a person is hit by an impaired driver and left with a multitude of physical injuries ranging from minor to life-threatening. What once was a daily routine is now filled with a rollercoaster of medical appointments as we work to heal our body and reassemble the pieces of our life. What injuries did you or your loved one sustain in the crash?

\*

JESSICA WEYER BENTLEY
Jessica was 5 when her 24-year-old father
Robert was killed by a drunk driver in 1979

I was not involved in the crash. My father was, and he was killed in the crash.

\*

SHANNON BOOS
Shannon was 20 when her 21-year-old brother
Kevin was killed by a drunk driver in 2015

My brother Kevin was killed instantly upon impact. The driver was speeding at approximately 100 mph in a 40-mph zone when he slammed into the passenger side of the car. Kevin's autopsy states that he was killed instantly. Kevin's two friends, Vincenzo and Morgan, were also killed. Morgan was pronounced dead soon after Kevin, however Vincenzo had a heartbeat for about two hours before he was pronounced dead.

The drunk driver walked away from the crash. Ran, actually. He was unable to be found for about forty-five minutes, and was eventually detained and brought to the hospital. He lived, of course.

The driver of my brother's car lived as well. After a few months of investigation, we were informed that while my brother and his two friends had little to no alcohol in their system, the driver was impaired. We will never know if this could have made a difference between literal life and death, and it haunts me every day.

*

TIFFANY COLSON
Tiffany was 30 when she was
hit by a drunk driver in 2011

My left foot and ankle were broken. The surgeon later told me that it was the same injury often seen in snowboarders and skiers. My right foot also had serious muscle and tissue damage. I was cut from head to toe. The airbag busted my nose so there was blood all over my face and shirt. I have healed as much as I can. I did have surgery seven months after the wreck to remove a piece of bone. I cannot be on my feet for more than four hours at a time or it starts to hurt and swell up. I had to really push myself to walk again. I was bedridden for a month and spent another month on crutches. It has been five years and I still have scars from the wreck.

\*

WENDY DAVIDSON
Wendy was 47 when her 28-year-old son
Chuck was killed by a drunk driver in 2016

I used to often wonder what if it was just "injuries" that my son suffered. How bad would it be? Would he be paralyzed? Would he have lived with brain injuries? Maybe just a simple broken leg or arm? Now I don't wonder the what ifs. It doesn't change the fact that my son has died, so all my what-ifs are gone. As I said before, I just couldn't bare seeing my son damaged. I don't regret not seeing him after his death. my last image of him is smiling and laughing and I desperately need it to stay that way. I'm afraid. I'm afraid of seeing those images but when the trial happens, I won't be leaving that courtroom. So, I have the painful task of preparing myself for what I might see. No mother should have to see their child so damaged. I hate it.

\*

BILL DOWNS
Bill's 21-year-old son Brad, 19-year-old daughter-in-law
Samantha, and 24-year-old family friend Chris
were killed by a drunk/drugged driver in 2007

Due to the death of my kids, none of them had any hospital time. My son was killed instantly due to blunt force trauma to the head and chest. The airbag failed to deploy, causing him to slam into the steering wheel. This shattered his ribs which punctured his lungs, killing him instantly.

Samantha, Brad's wife, didn't have a seatbelt on and was thrown into the dash. The engine of Brad's car exploded when the cars collided, and the other vehicle burst into flames. When the engine exploded, it was like a hand grenade and impaled Samantha into the seat of Brad's car, killing her instantly.

Chris was sitting in the back seat. He did not have his seatbelt on either, and was thrown forwards and upward, hitting his head on the roof of Brad's car which broke his neck. He still had a faint heartbeat at the scene, and was transported to the hospital but was dead on arrival.

*

JULIE DOWNS
Julie's 21-year-old son Brad, 19-year-old daughter-in-law
Samantha, and 24-year-old family friend Chris
were killed by a drunk/drugged driver in 2007

It breaks my heart to think that Brad, Sam or Chris suffered for one second. For days after the crash my mind wondered about that night, and I panicked at the thought of what they saw and how they might have suffered. The reenactment of the crash showed that Brad didn't swerve or brake at the time of impact. The coroner assured me that they didn't know what hit them, and that they died instantly. He even felt that Chris was already brain dead when they began transporting him to the hospital because of a faint heartbeat. He was dead on arrival.

Brad died from blunt force trauma to the head and chest. He had his seatbelt on but his airbag did not deploy. The steering wheel crushed his ribs which then punctured his lungs, but the head injury killed him instantly. The impact of the crash caused his brain to collide against the hard bones of the skull. He had a closed head injury so there was no visible evidence of a head wound. Both his legs were crushed and his left arm was broken. We don't know the full extent of his injuries. They did not do an autopsy because the drunk driver died in the crash, so no criminal charges would be filed. So all we have is Brad's death certificate and the information the coroner shared with us.

Samantha was on the side of the car that took the greater impact. Instead of taking the curve in the road, the drunk driver continued driving straight and crossed the center line. Her car hit my kids head-on, with the greatest impact being on the passenger side of both vehicles. Samantha wasn't wearing her seatbelt and was initially thrown forward and then backwards when the engine exploded in her lap, pinning her to the seat. Her airbag did not deploy either. Her internal injuries were massive, and she died from blunt force trauma to the head and chest.

Chris was the backseat passenger and also wasn't wearing a seatbelt. On impact, he was thrown up and forward, breaking his neck and almost every bone in his body. The only visible mark he had on him was a bruise on his forehead where the coroner said his brain exploded.

My kids did not have to die. If the drunk driver had made a better choice, they would still be alive.

*

MICHAEL GERSHE
Michael was 8-weeks-old when his 28-year-old
mother Barbara was killed by a drunk driver in 1970

The ambulance took the four of us to the same hospital to be treated, even though my brother didn't even have a scratch on him. My father suffered lacerations to his face and received stitches. The patrolman at the scene told the hospital to have a surgeon ready to treat my mother for her injuries. I am not sure how long she was in surgery for, but she died hours after the crash on the morning of September 20, 1970.

Nearly every bone in my body was broken, and my skull was fractured in the shape of a U. My injuries were so severe that I was airlifted to another hospital for treatment. My father told me years later that the doctors and even himself had no idea how I survived such severe injuries. My prognosis was touch and go. I was given countless blood transfusions to help keep me alive, and I still have the scars on my ankles.

Because of my injuries and since my bones weren't fully formed, I was put on a special board to heal. I had to be taken to the hospital for months afterward to make sure I didn't have any brain damage (while I don't have any, some of my friends may argue that point). As an infant, when I started to stand up, my father didn't think I was ready, but I was. When I started to walk, he remained worried, but I walked and then ran like any little kid at that age.

Despite the severity of my injuries, I healed and grew up to be a competitive swimmer. So whatever the doctors or a higher power did, it worked because here I am forty-six years later.

*

ANNETTE HANKS
Annette was 39 when she and her husband and their
13-month-old granddaughter were hit by a drunk driver in 2013

Thirteen-month-old Adilyn suffered two skull fractures and a brain bleed. She was in the pediatric ICU for three days. Wyatt had neck and back sprains. I had neck and back sprains, bone bruising on my wrist, and internal bruising. Physical injuries heal, but the emotional trauma that lasts a lifetime.

*

RENE LEDFORD
Rene's 25-year-old son Justin Colt
was killed by a drunk driver in 2015

Justin took the full blunt force of the crash. He had blunt force trauma to his head, face, neck, and torso. He had rib, clavicular and sternal fractures, a hemothorax, rupture of the pericardial sac around his heart, aortic and cardiac lacerations, pulmonary lacerations, multiple facial fractures, a deep cerebral contusion with intracranial hemorrhage, an open fracture of the larynx and trachea, laceration of the right jugular vein, a massive splenic laceration, soft tissue crush injury, left forearm, wrist and finger fractures and dislocations, comminuted and open fractures of the left fibula and tibia, and pulmonary anthracosis. In other words, Justin Colt's insides were crushed from to the impact.

His friend had multiple surgeries and stayed in the hospital for three weeks. Her left leg will never grow correctly, and she has to wear a special shoe.

*

LINDA PAULSON
Linda was 40 when her husband and their two
young sons were killed by a drunk driver in 2003

I was badly injured. I broke my left femur, left hip, right ankle, had a collapsed lung, damaged vertebrae, and had to have my spleen removed. I was in the hospital for six months. Because of the broken femur, I have a rod in my leg. I also had to have my hip replaced. My prognosis was good.

*

NICOLE RAMOS
Nicole was 32 when she and her two
children were hit by a drunk driver in 2013

After an hour and fifteen minutes, I was airlifted to the trauma center ten miles away. My ankle was crushed and the bones were sticking out of my skin. I had a broken wrist, a fractured and dislocated hip, three broken ribs, and three broken vertebra in my lower back.

My son had gashes on top of his head and the side of his face, and complained of stomach pain. He was airlifted to a children's hospital over two hours away. My daughter walked away with cuts, scrapes and severe bruising from the airbag and dashboard. I was in the hospital for twelve days, as was a passenger from the truck who hit us. A family of four was in the truck. The father sustained broken ribs and a collapsed lung. The mother had broken ribs, a broken hip, and a broken neck. Their three-year-old was airlifted to the same children's hospital as my son. They each stayed for two nights for observation. They also had a ten-day-old baby who was buckled in the baby carrier who didn't have a scratch.

\*

AMANDA RIDDELL
Amanda was 26 when she and her three
children were hit by a drunk driver in 2003

I had two fractured vertebrae in my cervical spine, and a bulging lumbar disc in my lower spine that was touching nerves. My daughter had seatbelt injuries.

\*

LINDSAY WELDON
Lindsay was 21 when she was
hit by a drunk driver in 2012

I was very fortunate. I had a few bruised ribs, a lot of facial trauma, a banged knee, and a really bad headache. I didn't require any surgery, but they did x- rays of my knee and ribs and a CT scan on my head and neck and I was examined for a possible traumatic brain injury. Everything came back clear so I was released from the emergency room about four hours later. I was the only one who had any injuries and there were no fatalities. My injuries weren't just physical. I now have anxiety and PTSD.

*

RACHAEL WILLIAMS
Rachael was 25 when her 30-year-old husband
Matthew was killed by a drunk driver in 2012

Matthew never made it to the hospital. He died instantly from his injuries. He broke his femur, both shins, both ankles, had bleeding from the brain, and severe blunt force head trauma.

*

SHELLY WOODWARD
Shelly was 30 when her 16-month old son was injured in a
drunk driving crash caused by Shelly's former husband in 1996

My son obtained a closed skull fracture and spent the night in observation. No one could give me a prognosis. I had to take time off work to watch him since he was so little, and make certain to guard his head.

*

HIT BY IMPAIRED DRIVER

We can start from nothing.
Whatever we have, wherever we are,
that is the place we can start from.

H.H. the KARMAPA

\*

---

# CHAPTER FOUR

# THE DRIVER'S CHARGES

The driver is safer when the roads are dry. The roads
are safer when the driver is dry. -UNKNOWN

Driving under the influence is a crime. Despite taking such huge risks including criminal charges and even death, impaired drivers continue to get behind the wheel. What happened to the driver responsible for your crash?

\*

JESSICA WEYER BENTLEY
Jessica was 5 when her 24-year-old father
Robert was killed by a drunk driver in 1979

In 1979, the laws were different than they are today. Drunk driving was not viewed as a crime but more as an accident. The offender did not receive jail time but we were able to prove in civil court that he was guilty and liable. He went on to reoffend and finally received jail time after hitting an Amish family in the 1980s.

\*

SHANNON BOOS
Shannon was 20 when her 21-year-old brother
Kevin was killed by a drunk driver in 2015

The impaired driver essentially walked away without a scratch. Although it's all a blur now, I do remember learning that he was conscious at the crash scene and ran away, hiding for forty-five minutes before he was found and brought to the hospital. The reports state that he was visibly intoxicated, shouldn't have been driving, and was on parole for another crime. This crash violated his parole, and was added to his charges.

The crash happened on September 6, 2015, but he wasn't arrested and charged until February 2016. While my family sat at a gravesite on Thanksgiving and Christmas with holes in our chests, the scumbag (this is the term my family uses, as we refuse to say his name) walked free and spent the holidays with his family.

The drunk driver is currently in jail awaiting trial, projected to take place in February 2017. I dread the day I see the face of the man who took my brother's life.

*

TIFFANY COLSON
Tiffany was 30 when she was
hit by a drunk driver in 2011

The drunk driver had a fractured skull and was hospitalized. I was in the trauma room when I found out that the other driver was drunk. A police officer came into my room and was carrying a large paper bag. I asked him how the other driver was, and the officer told me that the other driver was drunk. He then started to empty out the bag—it was full of pill bottles and liquor bottles. He said that when they opened the drunk driver's truck door, lots of liquor bottles fell out. I was shocked at first because I really didn't expect to hear that. I was raised in a very drunk and violent family, and I have chosen to stay away from people like that. I took the assault personally. It was like he had just slapped me in the face. Then I got mad, angry, and upset. There are not enough words to describe how I felt, and how I still feel some days.

\*

WENDY DAVIDSON
Wendy was 47 when her 28-year-old son
Chuck was killed by a drunk driver in 2016

The day I learned my son had died, I was told it was a drunk driver who caused the crash. At first I didn't comprehend what that meant until I learned the drunk driver was traveling down the wrong side of the highway when he hit my son. According to the police, it appeared that Chuck attempted to avoid the drunk driver.

The drunk driver went home from the hospital the next day with only minor injuries. He essentially stayed overnight for observation because of his intoxication. How was this even possible? The anger I felt toward this man who carelessly took my son's life because of his selfish act was immense, and it still is. This man is a murderer in my eyes. He may not have intentionally set out to murder Chuck, but he deliberately drank too much and then intentionally drove—therefore he is a murderer. The drunk driver went home while my son went to the morgue.

\*

BILL DOWNS
Bill's 21-year-old son Brad, 19-year-old daughter-in-law
Samantha, and 24-year-old family friend Chris
were killed by a drunk/drugged driver in 2007

I had gone to the hospital to identify Chris. Once my wife arrived and we were speaking with the coroner, we found out that the driver who killed our kids also died in the crash. At the scene they took blood samples from the driver and her passenger, who was ejected from their vehicle. The driver was traveling 80 mph at the time of the crash. The driver was impaired, drugged, and texting at the time of the crash. Her blood alcohol content was .012. She was partially ejected through her windshield and died instantly. Her passenger sustained a punctured lung, lost her spleen, and one leg was amputated. Both had spent the day drinking and partying at a local bar, and were still wearing bracelets from the bar at the time of the crash. When the coroner told us that the driver was believed to be impaired, drugged and had been texting, we were even more distraught. I became very angry and hated the driver, even though she died in the crash too.

*

JULIE DOWNS

Julie's 21-year-old son Brad, 19-year-old daughter-in-law<br>Samantha, and 24-year-old family friend Chris<br>were killed by a drunk/drugged driver in 2007

Brad was traveling 50 mph in a Ford Mustang and the drunk driver was traveling 80 mph in a Mitsubishi Endeavor when she crossed over into his lane. It was nighttime and she didn't have her headlights on. I believe that's why Brad didn't see her or have time to react. The drunk driver also died on impact. She didn't have her seatbelt on and was partially ejected onto the hood of her car as it burst into flames. A witness was able to pull her from the vehicle before she burned. Her passenger was ejected thirty to forty feet, and was found only when a paramedic tripped over her in the ditch. She survived but with permanent injuries. She lost a leg, a lung and her spleen.

We were told at the hospital hours after the crash that the driver of the Mitsubishi was drunk. From the moment I learned Brad was killed, until those words came out of the coroner's mouth, I was fearful that Brad had done something wrong. My fear turned into anger. The coroner assured me that Brad was not at fault in any way. This was the point when I knew my kids had been murdered.

Drinking and driving is not an accident. This lady made the choice to drink one beer after another, along with doing drugs; she was drunk and drugged. She was offered a safe ride home and turned it down, making the choice to get into her car and turning it into a weapon. She murdered my kids.

\*

MICHAEL GERSHE
Michael was 8-weeks-old when his 28-year-old
mother Barbara was killed by a drunk driver in 1970

I didn't learn that it was a drunk driver who hit us until I was in high school. I remember reading the press release my father kept in his bedroom cabinet when I was getting something out of there for him. Knowing it was a drunk driver changed my perspective on everything. I had always called it a car accident. Now it was a "drunk driving crash."

My emotions then and now range from sadness to anger, especially when I read the police report of that night. Knowing that the drunk driver had a revoked license and lied to the police will always anger me. He and his friends who were in the car with him claimed he wasn't driving. At the scene, they all stuck to the same story even though he was sitting in the front seat when the patrolman arrived on the scene. Fortunately, the officer noticed the smell of alcohol on his breath and notice his eyes were bloodshot, along with his slurred speech.

When another patrolman interviewed him at the hospital nearly three hours after the crash, he finally admitted that he was driving the car. His blood alcohol content nearly four hours after the crash was .10. He was arrested for drinking while intoxicated, reporting a false incident, and driving with a revoked license. Bail was set at six thousand dollars. He couldn't pay, so he sat in prison until the trial. While awaiting trial, he refused to plead guilty but finally pled guilty to the charge of negligent homicide. He was sentenced to three years in jail with time served.

Knowing the facts of what transpired does, in fact, anger me but I also know that being mad my entire life does not solve anything. I know that my mother would not want me to be angry because it's just an unhealthy way to live, so I try not to be — but there are times when I just can't help it.

*

ANNETTE HANKS
Annette was 39 when she and her husband and their
13-month-old granddaughter were hit by a drunk driver in 2013

I knew immediately something wasn't right. I made it clear that I wanted the other driver tested for drugs and alcohol. After we knew what Adilyn's injuries were and that she was being airlifted, we were told that the driver had been arrested for impaired driving. He had an open beer in his vehicle and blew .105 at the scene. I cried when I found out. I just knew something wasn't right about him.

*

RENE LEDFORD
Rene's 25-year-old son Justin Colt
was killed by a drunk driver in 2015

The drunk driver was put in jail and has stayed there since the crash. He took a "12 plea" on July 11, 2016. He is currently serving time in a Texas prison. He received eight years for intoxication manslaughter for the death of my son, four years each that run concurrently, intoxication injury to his friend, and two fleeing the scene charges. At first my family and I were very angry. But because of the young man my son was and the big heart he had, we knew he would want us to forgive, so we turned our anger into forgiveness.

*

LINDA PAULSON
Linda was 40 when her husband and their two
young sons were killed by a drunk driver in 2003

I found out that the driver was drunk a couple weeks after the crash. The driver was charged with only four counts of negligent homicide—misdemeanors. I was devastated.

*

NICOLE RAMOS
Nicole was 32 when she and her two
children were hit by a drunk driver in 2013

The impaired driver fled the scene on foot. When I learned that his car still smelled of alcohol at the wreckage yard three days later, I was appalled. Later that week the local news ran a story asking for leads on our hit and run. They said the driver hid in a pasture for three hours before he knocked on someone's door to use the phone so he could call for a ride back to his house. I became enraged when I found out that the drunk driver walked away from the scene, leaving behind four screaming children. This image haunted my dreams for a long time after the wreck. I felt overwhelmed that I couldn't spend the holidays with my children, suffered from chronic pain following multiple surgeries, while he out living his life as if nothing ever happened..

*

AMANDA RIDDELL
Amanda was 26 when she and her three
children were hit by a drunk driver in 2003

The driver was charged with many different things including failing to stop, impaired driving, speeding, and not wearing a seatbelt. The list of charges was a page long. I sued him through our insurance company. I don't know how I felt. I remember wanting to fight anyone and everyone who touched booze, I was so sick of this. Many times I hated him. I'm just glad I don't know who he is.

*

LINDSAY WELDON
Lindsay was 21 when she was
hit by a drunk driver in 2012

The impaired driver was arrested on the spot with a .21 breath alcohol content. I found out through my mom that he was drunk while at the hospital. I felt really angry.

*

RACHAEL WILLIAMS
Rachael was 25 when her 30-year-old husband
Matthew was killed by a drunk driver in 2012

The driver served a total of eighteen months. He finally took a Cobb agreement and was granted time served, allowed out of jail and put on probation for five years. I was very upset when I found out that the driver was drunk. My husband was no saint and the main reason for losing his license was drinking, yet he lost his life because the other driver needed to go for a ride. I have a lot of hate and anger toward him.

*

SHELLY WOODWARD
Shelly was 30 when her 16-month old son was injured in a
drunk driving crash caused by Shelly's former husband in 1996

He was given a DUI and went to court. We lived in the state of Ohio, where the laws weren't strict nor adhered to at the time. I was nice to him only so I could attend court. I knew he had prior arrests, but was shocked to hear the judge say that this was his fifth offense for driving impaired.

I wanted him to go to jail. I wanted a maximum sentence. At that time in Ohio, it was up to the judge to decide sentencing. He threw out all the prior arrests and put him in jail for eighteen days with a seven hundred dollar fine. His dad paid the fine, and for eighteen days he called me collect just to call me all sorts of names. His blood alcohol content, which they almost threw out of court, was .23 two hours after cutting him out of the car. I requested that they take his blood and in Ohio there had to be consent. I am glad they kept it to show him he was legally way beyond intoxicated.

\*

I have been brought up and trained to have the
utmost contempt for people who get drunk.

WINSTON CHURCHILL

*

# CHAPTER FIVE

# JUGGLING OUR EMOTIONS

Road sense is the offspring of courtesy and the parent of safety. -MAUD VAN BUREN

Being a victim of an impaired driving crash driver leaves us with intensely emotional wounds. Juggling pain with frustration, rage, fear, survivor's guilt, and more create a complex rollercoaster. Which emotions were hardest for you to manage in the aftermath?

*

JESSICA WEYER BENTLEY
Jessica was 5 when her 24-year-old father
Robert was killed by a drunk driver in 1979

My emotion was shock, fear, and grief. Even after so many years, I find myself fearing the nightmares and suffering the symptoms of PTSD. It is a constant process, though it has lessened some over time.

*

TIFFANY COLSON
Tiffany was 30 when she was
hit by a drunk driver in 2011

At first it was shock and disbelief. I could not grasp that this had happened to me. Then I got angry. It is not as intense as it was in the beginning five years ago, but I still get mad sometimes.

\*

WENDY DAVIDSON
Wendy was 47 when her 28-year-old son
Chuck was killed by a drunk driver in 2016

After hearing of the death of my son Chuck, I felt physically sick. The pain in my heart was unbearable. I couldn't breathe because the pain was so great. My stomach was in knots. It felt like the weight of the world had fallen on top of me. These emotions, to be honest, can't be expressed. There are truly no words to describe the immense and complete raw pain you feel when you lose a child.

Chuck was the oldest of my five children, my baby boy. When he was born, I realized how vulnerable in the world I became. I had him for twenty-eight years. I fed him, bathed him, loved him, laughed with him, and held him when he cried, even as a man. I was his mother and someone took him from me, from his family, took his life. There are no words that come close to this heartache. The intensity has changed, but the rawness remains.

As of this writing Chuck has been dead for just under two months. I still have days when the pain and hurt are as intense as the day I learned of his death. All it takes is a memory, a song, a smell, a mannerism that will take me back to that pain. I can only handle things in small increments. At first it was minute by minute, then hour by hour, and then week by week. The tenth day of every month will now be a month-to-month timeline. It's almost as if I'm counting backward. When he was born—day one, then it was one month, then he started walking at eighteen months, he was potty trained at twenty-three months, his first year, and every year thereafter until year twenty-eight. Now I count again but in reverse. It is crazy how time has become a cornerstone of my life now. I do nothing but count anymore.

*

BILL DOWNS
Bill's 21-year-old son Brad, 19-year-old daughter-in-law
Samantha, and 24-year-old family friend Chris
were killed by a drunk/drugged driver in 2007

Once the funeral was over, facing each day was an unbearable challenge. I seemed to get up in shock each morning not knowing how I was going to face the day. Once I got over the initial shock, the anger set in. It seemed as though I was angry at the impaired driver, my wife, God, everybody—including myself. What could I have done to save my kids from this tragic event in our lives? For four years the anger ate at me. It began to affect my marriage. After almost destroying my marriage; I tried to take my life. I believe that was the turning point for me. God kept me from ending my life, and after giving my life to God my feelings began to change. The anger seemed to melt away. I began reading my Bible again, my wife's prayers were never-ending and were the only thing that saved me from my spiral into darkness.

*

JULIE DOWNS
Julie's 21-year-old son Brad, 19-year-old daughter-in-law
Samantha, and 24-year-old family friend Chris
were killed by a drunk/drugged driver in 2007

Losing my kids has been one big rollercoaster ride of emotions, and just when I think the ride might be over, another emotion hits and the ride starts all over again. In the first year I suffered from daily panic attacks that left me lifeless. I feared everything. I felt like I was going crazy. My mind wandered to the crash and I panicked over the thought of what Brad, Samantha and Chris had to have gone through. I was told they died on impact, but just the thought that they suffered for one second was too much to bear. I was supposed to protect them and I felt like I let them down. They would not want to be dead and there was nothing I could do to change it for them. I begged God to let me trade places with just one of them. Why did all three of them have to die? I missed them so much. I tried to pretend that they were just away on vacation and that they would walk through the door and scream, "Surprise!" But that never happened.

I didn't know how to live without them. I was heartbroken, lonely, and spent my days crying. I longed to be with them. The second year was worse. I was stuck in my grief. Reality set in and I accepted the fact that they were not coming home. With that reality came anger. I have never hated anyone as much as I hated the drunk driver. I was glad she was dead. I felt that she got what she deserved but in her stupidity of driving after drinking, I wished she hadn't killed my kids. My emotions were out of control.

I was told that the drunk driver died in the crash, but I had to see her name on a headstone for myself. Bill and I searched through the cemeteries for her grave. It was like an obsession—I couldn't stop until I found it. The search seemed impossible. We knew the county where she was buried, but just didn't know which cemetery. It was an hour-and-a-half drive away, and we went every weekend to search. After about four weekends I finally called the funeral director who had helped us, and he was able to find out what funeral home she had been taken to. The next weekend we went to that funeral home and told a little white lie, saying that we were looking for a friend's grave because we wanted to pay our respects. We were afraid that if we told the truth, they wouldn't tell us where she was buried. They guided us directly to it. As I stood staring at her unkempt grave, I had an overwhelming feeling that if she were alive, I would kill her with my bare hands. I saw her as the devil himself. I cried so hard that I couldn't catch my breath. I made it to the car and sat there, and this feeling of hate and anger took over and I got back out of the car and spat on her grave. I swore that I would never forgive her for what she had done to my kids. I told her that death was too good for her.

I allowed the hate and anger to consume me. It ate at the very core of who I was. Life had no meaning for me and I cared about nothing. I knew I had another child, and I did what I had to do to care for her, but having her did not remove the pain of losing my son. I wanted both of them, not just her. I was grieving so deeply, but I continued to ignore the tug I felt from God and all I had believed in before the crash. I didn't want to be comforted nor feel any sense of peace that God could give me. I was mad at God for not saving my kids. So I suffered through each day hating life and trying to make sense of the pain that consumed me.

One day as I stood staring into the bathroom mirror, I realized I didn't know the person looking back at me—the person I had become. Although I knew he couldn't, but if my son were to return, he wouldn't know who I had become, and I wanted to be the person he knew. I had allowed hate and anger to control my life.

As I stood there, a glimmer of light shined through the fog I had been living in. It was a ray of hope. The intense emotions of my grief began to ease. The change in me after almost two years was gradual. I would turn on the radio and listen to Christian music. Sometimes the song playing would speak to my heart and I would angrily turn it off and cry. I was still fighting the comfort God was trying to give me. How could I let the hurt and anger go? I felt that in doing so, I would be letting go of my kids. I had to stay miserable. In continuing in life, I felt that I would be saying that it was okay that they were dead, and it wasn't okay. I didn't want to live without them.

I continued listening to Christian music, and Bill and I started going to church. I would sit there and fight the emotional turmoil going on inside me. I felt so vulnerable. God was leading me to forgiveness and I was fighting every step of the way. Bill came home from work one day, it had been almost two years since the kids were killed, and he found me crying. This wasn't unusual, but for me, this time it was different. A song that I had heard opened my eyes to God's love and I let Him take over my heart. I finally released the anger and was filled with a sense of peace that can only come from God. I made Bill listen to the song, and we held each other and cried. I thought that Bill was feeling the same, but he wasn't. He was still fighting his emotional war, and God wasn't winning. Releasing the anger and giving it to God set me on a healing path. I had been stuck in my grief, and I was finally able to take the first step out of the pain that had been consuming me.

*

MICHAEL GERSHE
Michael was 8-weeks-old when his 28-year-old
mother Barbara was killed by a drunk driver in 1970

Because I was an infant at the time of the crash, I really didn't start processing everything until my late teens, when I left for college. Growing up, I knew my mother was dead and would feel sad at times because she was not in my life. I've asked the what ifs many times throughout life, but since I don't remember the short eight weeks I had with her, I didn't know what I was really missing.

When I left for college, I started to process everything and noticed that sadness and anger were the most prevalent emotions. I found myself swimming mad, trying to take it all out on the water. I was mad at God, the man who killed my mother, and sometimes mad at my father for not talking about it more. I wasn't an angry person, but I used humor to deflect any depression I felt. I had guilt for surviving the crash because I felt that I was only an infant and my mother was twenty-eight and already had a life. All I did was eat, sleep, and fill up diapers, so why was I alive? These feelings subside at times, but never go away.

It can be hard to control the anger and sadness because they can consume a person's life. I use those emotions to motivate me to make a difference with the Magic of Life program. I just don't want others going through all of this pain. I learned that being angry and sad my entire life is a very unhealthy way to live and thank God I was blessed with a sense of humor which balances it all out. Besides, I don't think my mother would want me to feel this way. However, you just can't help it at times.

*

ANNETTE HANKS
Annette was 39 when she and her husband and their<br>13-month-old granddaughter were hit by a drunk driver in 2013

After the crash I made sure to attend court every single time the drunk driver had a scheduled appearance. I wanted him to see my face and to know that he didn't break us. In the courtroom, I was very strong and courageous, but outside of it I was a terrified, traumatized, heaping mess. I was scared to drive or ride in a car. I thought every car was going to crash into me. Countless times I had to pull over to cry because I was so scared. If I saw a lighted, blinking pedestrian crossing, I would have a panic attack. I couldn't stop at the pedestrian crossings for a couple of years, I would pull into a business parking lot until the road was clear.

To this day I still have some of this anxiety and terror, but it's not as bad as it used to be. I now have an amazing service dog who helps me so much. For a long time, I carried so much guilt knowing that it was most likely my head that hit my granddaughter and caused her injuries. I know it's not my fault, but there's still that little lingering guilt.

*

RENE LEDFORD
Rene's 25-year-old son Justin Colt
was killed by a drunk driver in 2015

Anger is the worst emotion my family and I have had. The emptiness of not having Justin Colt around is engulfing. His love is all around us. The pain of him being gone is still horrible. But our anger has changed into forgiveness, as the drunk driver did not make us have to endure the trial, and instead took the plea my daughters and I agreed on. Now it's the loneliness and the knowing Justin Colt is never coming back. He is physically gone, but spiritually here forever.

*

MELISSA MORIN
Melissa was 30 when she was
hit by a drunk driver in 2013

For me, it was fear, sadness, and anxiety which have improved a little with time. Anxiety is probably the thing that has stuck with me the most, and it's a terrible feeling. It hits more when I have to drive alone. I just can't seem to shake it. I have gone to the doctor for medication but I'm not a fan of prescription drugs, so I just deal with it and it has gotten better. I think it comes with the territory, so to speak. I went through a lot of trauma.

*

LINDA PAULSON
Linda was 40 when her husband and their two
young sons were killed by a drunk driver in 2003

Anger was, and still is, an emotion that I have trouble dealing with. I also dealt with a lot of survivor's guilt.

*

NICOLE RAMOS
Nicole was 32 when she and her two
children were hit by a drunk driver in 2013

Immediately after the wreck I was worried about work, bills, and my children. That all changed when I found out the crash was caused by a drunk driver who fled the scene and left all of us for dead. I became very angry, and focused on catching him and making him accountable for his actions but the investigator didn't have the same intentions. I started to feel rage when I found out that the driver wouldn't find justice at his doorstep.

I watched his actions through his public Facebook account and saw that he was out living life like nothing even happened. I wanted him to the feel the physical pain I was going through. I wanted him to worry about how to pay bills and prepare for the upcoming holidays while lying in a hospital bed. For the first six months I wanted to hunt him down and make him pay for what he did to us. I then sought counseling and shared my thoughts as well as my fears about going forward. This gave me an outlet to be honest, and I started to think about what I would actually say to the man who changed my life forever. This really got the wheels turning, and my outlook started to change.

*

JEWEL ROSE
Jewel was 39 when she and her family
were hit by a drunk driver in 2012

Yes, the emotion after the crash did scare me. It never ended, really. I was living and reliving it. Each time I closed my eyes, I could see the cliff to my right and my family behind me to my left. I can still see the overcast sky and hear my thoughts each time I close my eyes. They call it PTSD. I call it a normal reaction to extreme terror. I could do nothing for my family, I could not help my husband save my children and me. He had to do that all on his own. My prayer was answered and today I realize that God helped him save us that day. Do I still live in terror? Four years of therapy, prayer and counseling have helped. Can I handle the terror of that day? Yes. Does it ever leave? No. I have learned how to conquer my demons. The replay in my head is a memory of the past, no longer my present. I can live with my pain and sadness, and know that each day I am learning a new way of living.

*

LINDSAY WELDON<br>Lindsay was 21 when she was<br>hit by a drunk driver in 2012

Fear was definitely the most intense emotion. I was afraid to leave the house, afraid to sleep, afraid to be in white cars, afraid to drive at night or at all, afraid to drive alone. The intensity of my fear has definitely changed over time. I'm not scared to leave the house or be in a white car as long as I trust the person driving. Since I have some medication to help with the nightmares and PTSD, I'm not scared to fall asleep. I felt like, for a while, I had to control it. I needed to be brave for my sister, who was six at the time.

*

RACHAEL WILLIAMS<br>Rachael was 25 when her 30-year-old husband<br>Matthew was killed by a drunk driver in 2012

With this accident, I had a lot of guilt. I felt it was my fault, and still do to this day. I have been diagnosed with depression and PTSD. I have traumatic nightmares about Matthew's death. I had to reach out for help because I could no longer do it alone anymore.

\*

SHELLY WOODWARD

Shelly was 30 when her 16-month old son was injured in a
drunk driving crash caused by Shelly's former husband in 1996

I was embarrassed, angry and I felt like the worst parent in the
world. A mother is supposed to protect her cubs at all costs. I could
have stayed home that night. I should have divorced him long
before that. In the past, he was both verbally and physically abusive
to me, but never toward my kids. I guess in my mind, I never
thought he would cross that line.

\*

GRIEF IS
By Julie Downs

Grief is a continuation of love.
The more you love,
the more you grieve.

It's love that has no direction
so it flows from your eyes
and gathers in your heart.

Grief is love with no place to go.

\*

CHAPTER SIX

# BRAVING THE TRANSITION

It takes 8,460 bolts to assemble an automobile, and one nut to scatter it all over the road. -UNKNOWN

As we begin the transition of reintegrating back into life, some find comfort in a familiar routine while others seek solitude. The one commonality we're all faced with is determining the starting point that marks the transition from our old life to the new. When did you return to your usual routine?

*

JESSICA WEYER BENTLEY
Jessica was 5 when her 24-year-old father
Robert was killed by a drunk driver in 1979

I was very young and blocked it out by returning to normal daily life. I functioned pretty well except for issues with insomnia and nightmares. Those two things stayed with me, even though I blocked out a lot of what happened to my dad.

*

SHANNON BOOS
Shannon was 20 when her 21-year-old brother
Kevin was killed by a drunk driver in 2015

My father and mother were both incredibly strong for my brother and me, and very supportive of every decision we made.

Not just after Kevin died, but always. But I know how lucky I am to have such strong, involved parents, as it was much needed during this time.

They told both my brother Jeffrey and I that we could take our time. "Don't worry about work right now. Don't worry about school either. Take care of yourself, we will support you. Find what is going to help you the most. If working will help you, do it. If doing nothing will help you, do nothing."

I was the first one to leave our family after the funerals. I was home for about eight days and then decided to just pack my stuff up and head back to school in Gainesville, Florida, before I changed my mind. I was convinced that if I just ripped the bandage off and threw myself back into the world, it would work. I was proven wrong very quickly.

My mother left a couple of days after I did and headed back to her home in northern Florida. Jeffrey, my brother, was already living in south Florida, and returned to work around the same time. My dad stayed home with Jeffrey for another week or so and then returned to his home and work in Tucson, Arizona.

While I did return to Gainesville, I didn't actually return to life itself. I withdrew from classes and decided to enroll in one online class just to try to have some sort of responsibility, but even that proved to be too daunting. Every day I sat at the computer to start an assignment. And every day I got nothing done. So I withdrew from that as well.

Next, I tried to get a job. I ended up quitting two days later, knowing I would get fired if I kept showing up late or calling out of my shifts. But grief is unforgiving, and the world has no mercy upon the bereaved. I didn't really transition back into life. I made the mistake of diving headfirst back into the world, but my plan backfired.

I remember crying in my bed most days. On other days I was silent, unmoving, and not really present. My bed saw me more than anyone else did. Friends had returned to their lives and I guess I was expected to get on with mine, too. But I didn't know how to. I found it physically impossible to get out of bed. It felt like a boulder was sitting on my chest and I couldn't move, and I could barely breathe. I was a vulnerable soul lying in a queen size bed, and grief had swallowed me whole.

*

TIFFANY COLSON<br>
Tiffany was 30 when she was<br>
hit by a drunk driver in 2011

I was bedridden for a month. Then I was on crutches for a month. I did not return to work for six months after the wreck. I returned to work in September, but I ended up having surgery that December because of bone fragments that were from the wreck. I still have a limp to this day.

*

WENDY DAVIDSON<br>
Wendy was 47 when her 28-year-old son<br>
Chuck was killed by a drunk driver in 2016

I'm the type of person who has to push herself in everything. These days I've had to push myself mentally. I opted to return to work exactly one month after Chuck's death. I felt that if I could get through that day, I could conquer any day. I made it through. It wasn't pretty, but I did the entire day. I was almost afraid that I wasn't going to make it back to work at all, because I had a panic attack on my first attempt to drive after my son's death. I had to mentally force myself to drive. I started small, going around the valley, getting comfortable behind the wheel and then graduating to the highway. My employer has been wonderful in my transition back to work and I must admit I'm fortunate to have the opportunity to work from home when I'm having a bad day. I recognize that not every mother will have this luxury and my heart aches for them, I know it was tough for me, as I got nothing accomplished that day. I can't imagine having to go back right away and function as you were hired to do. Three days of bereavement for the death of a child just isn't enough.

\*

BILL DOWNS
Bill's 21-year-old son Brad, 19-year-old daughter-in-law
Samantha, and 24-year-old family friend Chris
were killed by a drunk/drugged driver in 2007

After four weeks had gone by, my vacation time and sick leave were used up and it was time to return to work. Other than facing the kids' death and having to identify Chris' body, going to work was the hardest thing I had to do. Going to work was a challenge I had to face. After being away from work for four weeks for the death of my kids, it was hard facing people again. Having to face my fellow employees was a hard transition for me. I had become a loner and found I worked better alone. Though my supervisor and fellow employees seemed to support me; all I wanted to do was be at home with what family I had left.

\*

JULIE DOWNS
Julie's 21-year-old son Brad, 19-year-old daughter-in-law
Samantha, and 24-year-old family friend Chris
were killed by a drunk/drugged driver in 2007

"Fake it until you make it." After burying a child, that is exactly what you have to do. Two months after the kids were killed I learned to put on a fake smile. My family and friends wanted me to be my old self; it was hard for them to understand that the person I had been died with my kids. So I pretended to be what they wanted me to be, but on the inside I was dying.

I felt like it was time for me to go back to work, or at least try. I worked with my family running a laundry service inside a laundromat, and they had been very patient with me by giving me the time off that I needed. They had been covering my shift, and it wasn't fair for them to have to work those extra hours.

On my first day, I cried all the way to work. I still couldn't drive by the crash site, so I had to go several miles around. I finally got there. My face was red and my eyes were swollen, but I was still determined to try to work. Bill came by to get Cindy after he got off work, and he stayed for a few minutes. I convinced him that I was okay, but I was lying. He left and I fell apart. I did what I had to do, but I couldn't get out of there soon enough. Thankfully, we were not busy so I was able to avoid the customers. When my shift was over, I locked up and made it to the car. I couldn't control the tears and I was so afraid. I remember backing out of the parking spot, telling myself to call Bill to have him come get me. But I kept going. I was driving aimlessly, not sure where I was or what I was doing. I was in a panic. My sister Sandy, realizing that I was late getting home, called to see where I was. I answered the phone wailing and not making any sense at all, telling her I didn't know where I was. She told me to pull over into a parking lot because it wasn't safe for me to drive. She then asked me to describe the things around me. Through the tears I told her. She knew the place, and she and my other sister rushed to where I was, miles away from where I should have been. Sandy drove me home, and from that point on, I never left the house unless someone was with me.

I didn't go back to work. It wasn't because I didn't want to—it was because I couldn't control the panic attacks that left me lifeless.

The emotional pain felt like a punch in the gut and I would double over in physical pain. It took me two years to finally build up my confidence to engage in life again.

*

MICHAEL GERSHE
Michael was 8-weeks-old when his 28-year-old
mother Barbara was killed by a drunk driver in 1970

I grew up being a survivor of a drunk driving crash, so it's very much of an ongoing process. I think growing up as a competitive swimmer really helped because it gave me a regular routine. Morning practice, school, afternoon practice, repeat. As an adult, there are days when I don't want to do certain things, and some days are tougher to get through. I always felt supported by family and friends even though I hide most of my emotions from them.

I don't want pity or for people to feel sorry for me, and I never use the crash or death of my mother as an excuse in life. There are many people who have it worse than me, some who are even in this book. My usual routine consists of trying to make someone laugh during the day, which helps me to find a sense of normality.

However, with that being said, the older I get the more I find myself becoming a hermit, as one friend calls it. I do seek solitude and find comfort staying home and away from people. There are times when I try to get out of my comfort zone and to meet new people, but it gets tiring having to explain things to strangers. My time on stage doing comedy or the program is probably where I feel the most at peace.

\*

ANNETTE HANKS
Annette was 39 when she and her husband and their
13-month-old granddaughter were hit by a drunk driver in 2013

My husband went back to work about seven days after the crash because we couldn't afford for him to be off work any longer. My days were full of doctor visits and court.

\*

RENE LEDFORD
Rene's 25-year-old son Justin Colt
was killed by a drunk driver in 2015

It took about a week for me to return to cleaning houses. My younger daughter and granddaughter went with me for the first month. My oldest daughter took two weeks. We still haven't fully adapted to our new norm. We spend more time together. Our daily routines have changed, as Justin Colt was always part of our daily routine. We talk to him but don't hear his beautiful voice, just silence. Not seeing him physically is emotional draining.

\*

MELISSA MORIN
Melissa was 30 when she was
hit by a drunk driver in 2013

It was about a good seven months after the crash when I returned to work. At that time, my anxiety was at its peak and I tried my best to hide it. Jill and I worked at the same place. Thinking of our work routine at break and lunch, and also the looks I got from coworkers because of the scars on my face were really hard. My butt-length hair had been cut off because of the broken glass. It was a lot for me to handle. I will forever be self-conscious. I had and actually do sometimes call in sick when my body aches. Some days are unbearable, and I lay in bed and cry. I feel like I'm entitled to those days.

\*

LINDA PAULSON
Linda was 40 when her husband and their two
young sons were killed by a drunk driver in 2003

I didn't work at the time of the crash. It took a year for me to return to my usual routine. I had a very good support system through the whole thing.

\*

NICOLE RAMOS
Nicole was 32 when she and her two
children were hit by a drunk driver in 2013

I was not able to return to work until I completed all of my surgeries and physical therapy. All in all, it took almost three years to get back to where we left off some time ago. I went back to work this past fall and was not sure I would be able to handle a full day, so my disability gave me three months to try it before I officially went back to full time. In the beginning, I was not sure I was going to be able to do it. I went home crying because I just felt like a failure and that I would not be able to handle the load and hours on my feet. I thought about giving up, but then I realized that my endurance was slowly getting better. In December, I committed to sticking with it and finish out the schoolyear. The administration was very understanding. They allowed me to transition into work and supported me through my tough days.

\*

JEWEL ROSE
Jewel was 39 when she and her family
were hit by a drunk driver in 2012

I did not return to work right away. I had years of therapy for both my brain injury and for PTSD. I lost several jobs because I requested accommodations. I am told this is not uncommon. The education field is a funny machine. As a special education teacher, I am to teach students that they can do anything they want. They can request accommodations, they can have help by the social service systems. Ironically, the very system designed to help those with disabilities refuses to employ anyone with a disability. The thought of being inconvenienced is too much, and it's easy for them to skirt the law because the disadvantaged don't have the funds to hire an attorney to defend them.

I do work now. But I am working for a small company that knows my background and is willing to help me through my learning phases. This company just happens to be run by my husband. I could not have asked for a better supporter. I am no longer in danger of severe depression and no longer in the mindset that I will just be disabled. Yet, it wasn't the government, coworkers or a great insurance plan who saved me. It was my husband who started a company that allowed me to work around my needs. I now work part-time with children in a school in another state.

Five years later I now help run a very busy company, work a part-time job, and advocate for those who cannot advocate for themselves. I also helped change school policy while I was healing. Not too shabby!

*

MICHAEL SMITH<br>Michael's 39-year-old brother Patrick<br>was killed by an impaired driver in 2007

I went back to work about two weeks after the accident. Coworkers and friends were supportive but I was, and sometimes still am, in a daze when I think about how it all happened. We were never contacted by the family or the impaired driver's attorney. I think that annoyed me the most. No flowers, nothing printed in the paper, no letter, nothing. From that point on I began to compile information about similar accidents and began to meet and communicate with families of similar crash victims.

I stayed mad for a very long time, about five years, to be exact. On the eve of the five-year anniversary, which was also the closure on the statute of limitations in Connecticut, I had what was probably a breakdown. I opened a bottle of Stoli vodka and finished it. The very next morning I had a voicemail from Donna Gore, a national advocate and host of Shattered Lives Radio, asking if I would be a guest on her show.

\*

LINDSAY WELDON
Lindsay was 21 when she was
hit by a drunk driver in 2012

I had to return to work one week later, on Black Friday, or I would be fired. I was still in intense pain and my face was still banged up. The transition was really difficult. I went from taking it easy and trying to heal to working a long, physically demanding shift. I had support from friends, family, and coworkers through this whole process.

\*

RACHAEL WILLIAMS
Rachael was 25 when her 30-year-old husband
Matthew was killed by a drunk driver in 2012

I was six months pregnant at the time. I did not return to work. I moved homes, and took on the responsibilities of being a single mother. After my baby was born, I had to go back to work. At first, I worked a few days a week and then eventually full time. I have cut down recently to three days a week because I felt I didn't get enough time with my children.

*

SHELLY WOODWARD
Shelly was 30 when her 16-month old son was injured in a
drunk driving crash caused by Shelly's former husband in 1996

I returned to work after a month-long leave of absence. My usual routine took a very long time to return to. My home, my Jeep and all the utilities were in my name, and I couldn't afford to pay them alone. My Jeep didn't have gap insurance, and the insurance company left me needing to pay five thousand dollars. I had to make payments on a totaled car, and buy another one so I could get to work every day. I had to file bankruptcy, which was humiliating since I had gotten myself established after my first divorce.

My family was there for me emotionally, but what could they say? No one was able to help me financially, and I didn't expect them to. At the time, no organization reached out to help me. Now that I know about MADD and other organizations, it makes me sad to think they didn't reach out to me.

*

I've come to understand that holding on to things
that are done against us only hurt us more.

JULIE DOWNS

*

# CHAPTER SEVEN

# FINDING SUPPORT

*Words of kindness are more healing to a drooping heart than balm or honey. -SARAH FIELDING*

Despite an aftermath that is best described as chaotic, many victims and their families are left to their own devices. Following the crash, what resources were offered to help you handle the trauma?

\*

JESSICA WEYER BENTLEY
Jessica was 5 when her 24-year-old father
Robert was killed by a drunk driver in 1979

It was 1979, and things worked differently back then. I can say that law enforcement, emergency personnel, and witnesses supported my dad to get him the help he needed. They also stopped the impaired driver from running from the scene. I am thankful for them daily, that my father was not alone.

\*

TIFFANY COLSON
Tiffany was 30 when she was
hit by a drunk driver in 2011

I was given some business cards and told to look up MADD. No one really offered me any help, though.

\*

WENDY DAVIDSON
Wendy was 47 when her 28-year-old son
Chuck was killed by a drunk driver in 2016

My family was not offered help, or resources for counseling, group counseling, or access to victim advocates as far as I'm aware. We were given contact information for the police officers who were handling the investigations, and that's it. When you see glimpses of death on the news or read about it in the newspaper, to many it's nothing more than tragic news of the day and they move on. You never think you are going to be the headline. It is nothing that anyone will ever imagine going through, nor want to, when it comes to your children. It's almost taboo to even give it a thought.

When it happens to you, everything changes in an instant. You realize that you and your loved one have now become a statistic. You become hypervigilant with all news stories, and knowing the whereabouts of your children and family. Your whole perspective on things going on in the world immediately changes. What once was important is no longer. You realize that life is too short to do things you don't like doing. It's all so damn cliché, but it all true.

There is a reason counselors tell you not to make any drastic decisions within the first year of tragic loss. You become desperate to do anything you can to dull the intensely raw pain. It can become almost an obsession to do whatever it takes just to breathe again. As I said earlier, you learn to take time in small increments. You tell yourself that if you can just get through the next five minutes, you'll be okay. Maybe.

*

BILL DOWNS
Bill's 21-year-old son Brad, 19-year-old daughter-in-law
Samantha, and 24-year-old family friend Chris
were killed by a drunk/drugged driver in 2007

We were not offered any type of support by law enforcement or anyone else. When we found out the driver had been impaired, we tried contacting the local MADD office but were told they could not help us due to lack of resources. We did find a local support group from a church, but were otherwise on our own.

I think the most traumatic experience I live with is knowing I was just moments from seeing my kids lying on the payment that night if law enforcement hadn't detoured everyone around the crash site. I want to tell others who experience this loss that you must face this nightmare. You must go through it — you cannot go around it or over it. You must live through it. It will get easier over time, but you cannot change the past and your loved one would want you to keep going.

*

JULIE DOWNS
Julie's 21-year-old son Brad, 19-year-old daughter-in-law
Samantha, and 24-year-old family friend Chris
were killed by a drunk/drugged driver in 2007

We were left to ourselves to find support and resources after the crash. The hospital did not offer any, but that could have been because neither Brad nor Samantha made it there; they went straight to the morgue. Chris went to the hospital but we weren't legally his next of kin, so we had no say other than Bill identifying his body. The only encounter we had with law enforcement was when we picked up the crash report. They were very helpful in answering our questions about the crash, but they never offered assistance to help us find support. The coroner did meet us at the hospital and stayed with us for several hours, but never asked if we needed someone to talk with. The only support that the funeral home offered was in the burial planning. It would have been nice if one of them had a referral list of organizations who offered support.

We found our support through family and friends. Our pastor, without our calling him, showed up and we were able to lean on him. Our families were also there for us. My sister Sandy called and found a support group for homicide victims, and we went to a few meetings but had a hard time fitting in because their tragedies were different from ours. Their loved ones had been murdered using guns and knives, and some had even been raped. We called our state MADD office, but they were not able to help us. Four years after the crash when our marriage was in shreds because of the extreme pain of losing the kids, we sought counseling through a local church.

*

MICHAEL GERSHE
Michael was 8-weeks-old when his 28-year-old
mother Barbara was killed by a drunk driver in 1970

I don't remember what age I was told about the car crash and my mother, but I do recall feeling stunned. My father told me numerous times that I looked like "a bowl of Jell-O," and I remember feeling overwhelmed knowing I had almost died. I didn't understand the magnitude of it as a kid, but it's pretty heavy on the emotional level, to say the least. I was grateful to be alive but knowing my mother was dead was quite hard to grasp. Even today, it's sometimes hard to understand the why of it all.

Growing up, I did not go to therapy; I'm sure no one thought it was necessary. I never really spoke about it as a kid other than writing "deceased" where my mother's name would be on school form. I just spent my days being a kid, whether it was swim practice, school, playing with Star Wars toys, performing magic, or just reading comic books. It wasn't until I was older when I realized just how lucky I was to be alive and began to understand how precious life can be. I remember speaking at a conference in western Pennsylvania when a teacher called me "a miracle." That comment still blindsides me.

I was too young to remember any details from the crash, and for that I am grateful. However, the aftermath of the experience lives on every day. I had the physical trauma as an infant and overcoming all those injuries, but I think the mental aspect of it is the toughest. I could not imagine being an adult and going through the injuries one might suffer from after being hit by a drunk driver. Having the support from the people I care about and the ability to share my story is, I believe, way more valuable than what counseling could do for me. Each person handles a traumatic experience differently, but I really believe the mental recovery is the hardest.

*

ANNETTE HANKS
Annette was 39 when she and her husband and their
13-month-old granddaughter were hit by a drunk driver in 2013

We didn't get help from anybody. We had to learn how to deal with all this new stuff on our own. It was very scary. I had no idea someone could have posttraumatic stress from a car crash. I thought it was only for war veterans. I didn't know much about it. So when I was having debilitating panic attacks in my car because someone didn't slow down soon enough, I felt like I was going crazy. After suffering every single day for a couple of years, I decided to research PTSD. I just don't understand why nobody talked to us about what happened. Nobody suggested that we go see a counselor or pastor. No help at all. We suffered together in silence. I want anybody who is reading this to know that there is help. If you feel that you are suffering from PTSD, please reach out to someone.

*

RENE LEDFORD
Rene's 25-year-old son Justin Colt
was killed by a drunk driver in 2015

We were offered support but declined at first. We are now part of an organization, Stop DWI, founded by a husband and wife who lost their twenty-four-year-old son to a drunk driver in 1984. They work closely with judges, law enforcement and city officials. Drunk, drugged and distracted drivers are court-ordered to attend monthly meetings set up by Stop DWI so they can hear statements given by victims and their families. They hold seminars at schools to bring more awareness about the dangers of drunk, drugged, and distracted driving. Stop DWI also attended every court hearing we had. They do this with all families in our situation in Midland, Texas, and surrounding areas in west Texas. They have been our biggest support and are part of our family now.

I have since decided to start counseling. I feel as though I'm stuck. I know I will always miss Justin Colt and wish he were here, but sometimes I need to get my feelings out. I'm not angry at the drunk driver, but I'm angry at the choices he made that night.

*

MELISSA MORIN
Melissa was 30 when she was
hit by a drunk driver in 2013

The hospital had a lady come in to ask me questions and offer resources, but my injuries were so bad that we all knew it would take months for me to physically heal. I concentrated so much on getting physically healed that I didn't deal with the emotional part. It ultimately hit me like a freight train.

*

LINDA PAULSON
Linda was 40 when her husband and their two
young sons were killed by a drunk driver in 2003

I went for counseling. The fact was that my kids were gone and I didn't know how to deal with that. The thing about a highly traumatic experience is that you can't rush through the feelings no matter how much they hurt. Also, many of the same feelings will come back to you over and over.

*

NICOLE RAMOS
Nicole was 32 when she and her two
children were hit by a drunk driver in 2013

I was not offered resources by law enforcement to help handle the trauma of the wreck. My investigating officer never even interviewed me. I did not find out about crime victim funding until I contacted MADD about six months after the wreck. They got me in touch with counseling to help with nightmares and the emotional feelings that haunted me day and night.

I was completely blindsided by the fact that my car and medical insurances would not pay for anything because the drunk driver hadn't yet been caught, so they were all pointing fingers trying to figure out who would pay the bills. In the meantime, the bills came to me and I went into a very dark place, unsure about my future finances.

\*
JEWEL ROSE
Jewel was 39 when she and her family
were hit by a drunk driver in 2012

No. Not in the least. The state patrolman was wonderful but we did not have any more interaction from him after that day.

I had to testify to put the fifth-time drunk driver behind bars. The judge was going to put him on work release! The records show he only has four DUIs because of plea deals. He was supposed to go to counseling, but never has. The records don't show that the driver has two other DUIs in another state. The state patrolman did everything he could to get this guy off the street.

Testifying was one of the hardest things I had to do. I remember catching my breath and very slowly speaking about my sons running to save the man who hurt them. I testified how their training from Boy Scouts of America enabled them to be fantastic first responders. They should have been honored as heroes, but I didn't have the ability to fill out the paperwork to honor scouts in action. We were too busy trying to get this guy off the streets, helping our children heal when the school refused to help them, and finding a good doctor to help make decisions about when they should return to school.

No, we did not get much help or support from agencies. But we did get great support from my family. My husband's parents dropped everything and moved from three hours away to take the kids to their appointments so I could keep working; we needed my health insurance to pay for the specialists the kids needed. My in-laws also offered moral support since my mother spent every waking moment caring for my father who was battling cancer. My family who lived far away sent care packages, and nearby family came over and spent time with me as much as they could.

My sister-in-law made me get out of bed after I lost my job. That very same day I had to testify in court to send the driver to jail. The loss was crushing. I did not know how I was going to help my sons now. Everything I had worked for was gone, and I felt like I had let my family down. I was not supporting my husband, and felt completely useless.

At the time, it felt like my family would be better off without me. I truly felt that. For anyone who was or is suicidal as I was, that feeling made so much sense. If it hadn't been for my sister-in-law and her belief in me and helping others given to her by God above, I would not be here today.

What blindsided me the most was the fact that I knew the Family Medical Leave Act gave me the ability to attend 504 meetings for my son as well as doctor appointments for him and myself. Yet, human resources said that was only for people who were in the hospital or very near death.

I was also blindsided by my former boss and his behavior regarding the care of my son. He denied doctor recommendations, stating that schools don't have to follow doctor recommendations. He denied receiving them as well. He refused to honor school absences that allowed my son's brain to heal. At the same time, my then-current boss made it very clear I was not allowed to take any time off from work. I was told by one of my supervisors, "They don't like it when you are gone."

The title of my boss at that time was elementary school principal. The title of my former boss was high school principal. He even won Principal of the Year. He hurt my son and so many others but because I was hurt, I couldn't access the complaint system. He got away with cleaning files and harassing my son, and is now living well with a healthy retirement.

*

LINDSAY WELDON
Lindsay was 21 when she was
hit by a drunk driver in 2012

I wasn't offered resources or help to handle trauma from the crash. I took it upon myself to reach out for help. I was completely blindsided by MADD. They claim to be a voice for victims and survivors. They claim to be there around the clock for victims and survivors to have someone to talk to, attend court with, and to help write victim impact statements. They don't do that. It wasn't until Bill Downs from AVIDD reached out to me that I finally found support by others who have gone through the same thing. They're there for us through everything, around the clock. Bill and Julie Downs are one hundred percent true to their word. They make it possible for us to have a voice, to find support, and make friends with others who have experienced the same thing.

I want readers to know that a highly traumatic experience isn't all physical. There's a mental aspect as well. Even though you may be physically alone in a trauma, there's a world of support available by others who know what you're going through. Don't be afraid to reach out for help.

*

RACHAEL WILLIAMS
Rachael was 25 when her 30-year-old husband
Matthew was killed by a drunk driver in 2012

No, I wasn't offered anything. The detectives gave me only the number to the coroner's office and their cards. It wasn't until after Matthew's funeral that the owner of the funeral home gave me a bunch of material including groups for grieving. I felt that the court proceedings I attended were just a waste of time, and full of empty promises. I endured eighteen months of torture only to watch the driver be released and hear the judge say, "I'm sorry things happened the way they did." I would never wish this on anyone, and laws should be stricter when it comes to drunk driving.

\*

SHELLY WOODWARD
Shelly was 30 when her 16-month old son was injured in a
drunk driving crash caused by Shelly's former husband in 1996

No one offered me any support whatsoever. The only people who were there for me was my family. I was embarrassed about the incident but it was printed in the local newspaper and his family was well known. We lived in a small community where everyone knows everyone. I knew that people in the town were already aware. Our church families were very close, but none of the churches offered to help me.

\*

No person should suffer the tragedy of losing
someone as a result of drunk, drugged, or
distracted driving, but for far too long the danger
of impaired driving has robbed people of the
comfort of knowing that when they or a loved one
leaves home they will return safely.

BARACK OBAMA

\*

# CHAPTER EIGHT

# LEARNING THE CONSEQUENCES

The consequences of your life are sown in what you do and how you behave. -TOM SHADYAC

The dictionary defines consequences as a social, moral, and legal result or effect that arise from one's action or condition. What legal consequences did the impaired driver face in the crash aftermath?

*

JESSICA WEYER BENTLEY
Jessica was 5 when her 24-year-old father
Robert was killed by a drunk driver in 1979

The impaired driver did not face criminal charges in my father's death, but did face a civil suit. My mother and grandfather attended the hearing for this. The driver eventually faced charges for another impaired driving crash when he hit an Amish family, and had to spend time in jail.

I don't feel our case was handled appropriately, but this is largely due to the fact that the laws were different then. They are stricter now. I am very upset, of course, that this man did not do time for killing my father. If he had, the second crash may never have happened.

\*

TIFFANY COLSON
Tiffany was 30 when she was
hit by a drunk driver in 2011

Yes, the driver did face the charge of vehicular assault while under the influence. He was given five years in prison, and served three and a half years.

\*

WENDY DAVIDSON
Wendy was 47 when her 28-year-old son
Chuck was killed by a drunk driver in 2016

The drunk driver who killed my son has not yet faced charges, which is difficult to accept. When Chuck's father and I went to pick up Chuck's personal effects from the police department and to meet with the investigating officer, we were told that the department didn't want to press charges until after the investigation. As it was explained to us, the officer in charge felt it was better to wait until they were done with their investigation, to ensure that the proper and accurate charges were handed down. The explanation was that they didn't want to charge this man with DUI unless the investigation could show negligence, and then they could charge him accordingly and accurately.

Chuck's father and I agreed to be patient, but to this day we are still waiting to hear from the police that this individual has been charged. My son has been gone just over four months now, and still no charges have been filed.

I'm terrified that my son's life will be worth only four months in jail, or worse yet—nothing but probation. How is it that a murderer, who maybe didn't intentionally kill someone but was neglectful, can get a mandatory twenty years while a murderer with a car who is also negligent gets only four to seven years? We have to start changing the way we think about drinking and driving fatalities. It is a preventable crime. When will people realize that it's murder? We continue to try to be patient.

\*

BILL DOWNS
Bill's 21-year-old son Brad, 19-year-old daughter-in-law
Samantha, and 24-year-old family friend Chris
were killed by a drunk/drugged driver in 2007

The impaired driver was also killed in the crash, so there was no trial or court proceedings.

\*

JULIE DOWNS
Julie's 21-year-old son Brad, 19-year-old daughter-in-law
Samantha, and 24-year-old family friend Chris
were killed by a drunk/drugged driver in 2007

Because the drunk driver also died in the crash, we never had our day in court. She did not have her seatbelt on, and was partially ejected from her vehicle, killing her instantly. Her car burst into flames but she was pulled from the vehicle before she burned. She did pay the ultimate price for her crime, so I feel a sense of justice.

In our court system, too many times justice is not served for the crime against victims and families. The impaired driver receives a slap on the hand while the victim or their family receives a life sentence. The time served should match the crime. When a person makes the choice to drive impaired, he or she turns that vehicle into a weapon. Drinking and driving is a choice. Drunk drivers are nothing more than murderers.

*

MICHAEL GERSHE
Michael was 8-weeks-old when his 28-year-old
mother Barbara was killed by a drunk driver in 1970

The driver was charged with criminal negligent homicide, false reporting of an incident, operating a vehicle while intoxicated, and operating a vehicle with a suspended licensed. Obviously I was too young to attend or remember the trials, but there was a criminal and civil case against the driver. My grandfather was smart and kept my father away from the drunk driver throughout the trials, which was probably a good thing. This was back in 1970, so things have changed quite a bit when it comes to drunk driving and the justice system. However, while the drunk driver remained in jail awaiting trial, he kept pleading not guilty. He eventually plead guilty when the trial occurred.

I was in my thirties when I was able to obtain the report from the police department, and it upset me even more. Reading that the driver and his friends lied to the police was tough, and it made me want to find him. I understood why my grandfather kept my dad away from the driver during trial. After reading all the information, I couldn't help but get upset not only at him, but at the fact that he was sentenced to only three years in jail, with time served.

*

ANNETTE HANKS
Annette was 39 when she and her husband and their
13-month-old granddaughter were hit by a drunk driver in 2013

Our drunk driver's initial charges included vehicular assault while under the influence, driving under the influence, two counts of reckless endangerment, and driving while license suspended, revoked in the third degree. The court wanted to offer him a plea deal. A lot of thought went into our decision and we had three stipulations if a plea were to be offered. We wanted him to have a felony, Department of Corrections community custody, and treatment. He was twenty-nine years old and he already had a one felony, eleven misdemeanors, and a DUI on his record. We knew he needed help rather than just throwing him in jail.

The driver could have received thirteen years for the initial charges. The prosecution worked the plea with our stipulations, and the only way they could guarantee them was if they offered a first-time offender waiver. We struggled with that one. So they offered him a plea deal of one count of vehicular assault with disregard for the safety of others, a class B felony, and one count of reckless driving with willful or wanton disregard. The maximum sentence for those was ninety days.

We went to court for the plea and sentencing, and the driver was released the next day after serving seventy-six days in jail, fifteen days for time served. We felt pressured to offer the plea. The prosecutor was trying to convince us that if it went to court, the driver would be let go. So we were desperate. We like to help people and we wanted to see him get help, so that's why we agreed to the waiver.

We feel like we were thrown under the bus. We do not feel that justice was served. Three years after the crash I received a copy of the investigation and discovered damning information we were never told which surely would have sent the driver to prison. We feel lied to and used by the prosecutor and the justice system.

*

RENE LEDFORD
Rene's 25-year-old son Justin Colt
was killed by a drunk driver in 2015

We attended the pretrial and all four final pretrials due to postponements. At the fourth and final pretrial, the drunk driver took the twelve-year plea deal that my daughters and I agreed to.

*

MELISSA MORIN<br>
Melissa was 30 when she was<br>
hit by a drunk driver in 2013

I think the case went as expected. Of course the driver dragged it out for as long as he could. At the first court appearance, my heart was pumping because that was the first time I had ever seen him. I was overwhelmed with emotions. After that it wasn't so bad. I didn't attend every court date due to work and the fact that I lived at least an hour away. The prosecutor would usually contact me and let me know when it would be just another continuance. We all agreed to a plea deal which the driver ultimately took. He was sentenced to ten years and might serve five if we're lucky.

I'm glad I was able to do an impact statement. I wasn't able to write down my feelings, it was easier for me to just say whatever came to me. Ultimately, at the end of the day, it will never be enough time. It won't fix us, and it won't bring Jill back. There is no justice on that.

*

LINDA PAULSON<br>
Linda was 40 when her husband and their two<br>
young sons were killed by a drunk driver in 2003

The driver died but the car belonged to the passenger who gave his friend the keys to drive after they had been drinking all night. There was no trial and the case was handled very poorly. The passenger was charged with four counts of negligent homicide, which are only misdemeanors. He did ten months in county jail. I feel very let down by the justice system.

\*

NICOLE RAMOS
Nicole was 32 when she and her two
children were hit by a drunk driver in 2013

My drunk driver did not face charges. He wasn't even brought in for questioning. His face and first name were plastered in the local media asking for information of his whereabouts, but nothing ever happened after that. My officer did not even interview me. He had one statement from the truck driver who hit me head-on and was rear-ended by the drunk driver. When I received the crash report, it was not accurate and I went into a downward spiral. Apparently the truck driver slammed on his brakes, "brake checking" the car that was tailgating him. The car couldn't control his speed, swerved, and hit the rear passenger side of the truck. The truck started to spin and then entered my lane and hit us on the front driver's side. The truck driver tried to cover up his actions by stating that a car came into his lane and that's why he had to slam on his brakes. This statement was inaccurate because no one was in front of me, and I had just made a safe left turn onto the roadway. I was still accelerating to get up to the speed limit when they came over the hill.

I tried to give law enforcement several leads about the drunk driver's whereabouts. They finally told me that no one could place the driver behind the wheel at the time of the crash. A few weeks later they dropped my case. The investigator never even visited me or asked about my injuries. I was sickened by the fact that the only reason they didn't pursue him was because I did not die.

\*

JEWEL ROSE
Jewel was 39 when she and her family
were hit by a drunk driver in 2012

Yes, the driver faced charges but only because I testified. I had to testify to put him in prison for two years. Yet it was the testimony of my father-in-law that really made the difference to the judge. "No one is safe while he is on the road," was the quote that rang through my ears. Thankfully, my husband had taken many photos that showed the damage. The photos coupled with my testimony and that of my father-in-law put the guy away.

*

LINDSAY WELDON
Lindsay was 21 when she was
hit by a drunk driver in 2012

I attended all court dates, one of which the driver didn't show up for. He was charged with attempted murder with a deadly weapon, and felony DUI with injury to another person. He served five months in the county jail. He had a suspended driver's license for three years and was on probation for five years. This was his fifth DUI.

*

RACHAEL WILLIAMS
Rachael was 25 when her 30-year-old husband
Matthew was killed by a drunk driver in 2012

The driver faced four charges and later on a habitual offender charge. This was his third drunk driving offense. The first court proceedings were long and agonizing. We didn't get bounced over to circuit court until August 9, 2012. From there we went through many things. They tried to say that the driver wasn't read his rights, but he was—all four times he was questioned. The driver then fired his attorney and had to start all over again. He agreed to a Cobb's plea which would let him out of jail. He was sentenced to time served of eighteen months, five years of probation, and was required to wear an alcohol tether for a year. I did not like this outcome. My husband received no justice. The driver still has his family, still goes to work every day, and he still lives a normal life. All while mine is ruined.

*

SHELLY WOODWARD
Shelly was 30 when her 16-month old son was injured in a
drunk driving crash caused by Shelly's former husband in 1996

He did face charges in a local court. He was a five-time offender which I found out when I attended court. I begged the police officer to take his blood at the hospital. In Ohio, at that time you needed consent, which my ex-husband didn't give me. His lawyer wanted the blood alcohol content level thrown out. I was fearful they would discover I was the one who requested it, but they never did. I am glad they kept it on his record, because without it he would still maintain his denial of not drinking that night. The outcome, what he received for what he had done, pissed me off. He was supposed to be charged with child endangerment which was never brought up. To spend eighteen days in jail and be allowed to call me even with a restraining order in place, and then walk away was unfair to me and my child.

*

While an unimpaired driver can respond quickly
to changes in traffic and begin braking within
half a second, a legally drunk driver needs
an additional 4 feet to begin braking—
and a driver who's texting needs 70.

VIRGINIA TECH TRANSPORTATION INSTITUTE

*

# CHAPTER NINE

# LEGAL RAMIFICATIONS

The sensitivity of men to small matters, and their indifference to great ones, indicates a strange inversion. -BLAISE PASCAL

Depending upon local law and the facts of the case, the legal ramifications and the outcome for the impaired driver can vary widely. Do you feel that the driver faced the correct consequences? Where is the driver today?

\*

JESSICA WEYER BENTLEY
Jessica was 5 when her 24-year-old father
Robert was killed by a drunk driver in 1979

I do not feel that he faced the correct consequences. He received no time for killing my father. The man who killed my father is alive and well, living in the same town.

\*

TIFFANY COLSON
Tiffany was 30 when she was
hit by a drunk driver in 2011

Today he is free and lives in a town close to me. I do not know anything about his life in the present, nor do I care to. It would keep me in a hateful mood. I wish he would have been given the maximum sentence and had to serve it all. His personal life at that time went down the drain. He lost his family and was left all alone. So in the end he lost more than his freedom.

*

WENDY DAVIDSON<br>Wendy was 47 when her 28-year-old son<br>Chuck was killed by a drunk driver in 2016

When I did my research on Delaware law, I found the different forms of charges that can be applied to individuals who drink and drive and kill someone. I found that the most the police could charge this man with was second degree murder, and only if they could prove negligence on the driver's part. As of now, I don't know what constitutes negligence in this case, but the mandatory minimum is fifteen years in prison for second degree murder.

Personally, I feel that nothing will ever be good enough. The charges to individuals who get caught drinking and driving are pretty meek at best. Delaware does have a law that after your first conviction of DUI you are required at your own expense to install a car breathalyzer. This means your vehicle will not start if your blood alcohol content is above the legal limit of .08. Unfortunately, and sadly for my son, the driver's previous DUI occurred prior to this law taking effect.

I recently learned there is a car device that can be installed during manufacturing that detects a driver's blood alcohol content through biometrics, and prevents the car from starting if the driver is intoxicated. One death by a drunk driver is too many, as the death is completely and utterly avoidable. My son would still be alive today if this individual had not made the poor choice to drink and drive.

*

BILL DOWNS
Bill's 21-year-old son Brad, 19-year-old daughter-in-law
Samantha, and 24-year-old family friend Chris
were killed by a drunk/drugged driver in 2007

I believe the driver faced the ultimate justice. Due to her death, we also received a sense of justice. The driver is buried in Hope, Mississippi, just two hours from our home.

*

JULIE DOWNS
Julie's 21-year-old son Brad, 19-year-old daughter-in-law
Samantha, and 24-year-old family friend Chris
were killed by a drunk/drugged driver in 2007

I feel a sense of justice because the drunk driver also died in the crash. I can't imagine her surviving when she had killed my kids. I feel that she got what she deserved but I hate that she took my kids with her. Drunk driving is not an accident. It is a conscious choice, a very selfish, stupid choice. It is a crime that is one hundred percent preventable. A better choice can be made.

*

MICHAEL GERSHE
Michael was 8-weeks-old when his 28-year-old
mother Barbara was killed by a drunk driver in 1970

The victim/survivor never believes that the drunk driver gets enough punishment. However, back in 1970, sentencing the driver to three years was probably what the law stated. But then again, I just read about a twenty-year-old drunk driver who killed someone and only received three years!

Of course I wish that the driver had been sentenced to more time in jail. I feel that twenty-eight years, which was my mother's age, would have been enough punishment. I think it is hard to ask a crime victim what enough punishment is, because there is so much emotion involved. I think all of us would want life in prison or the death penalty.

I am not sure where the driver is today, as he would be in his seventies. Over the years I've had friends in law enforcement try to find him but they always came up empty. In my early twenties, if I had found him I would have confronted him, and probably done something stupid that landed myself in jail. As I get older, the anger doesn't necessarily lessen, but more jail time for him wouldn't have brought back my mother. I just wish he would have done more time in jail as punishment.

On May 25, 2016, I was presenting at Minot Air Force Base when one of the airmen asked what I would say to the drunk driver if given the chance. This is a question that I've been asked many times over the years, both by audience members and myself. However, on the day the airman asked this question, it happened to be my father's birthday, and I had a rare emotional meltdown on stage in front of two hundred American heroes. I heard the words of what I wanted to say echo through my brain, but they just wouldn't come out. I avoided eye contact and turned my back for a few seconds to regain composure. When I turned around to answer his question, my voice cracked and my eyes filled with tears as I said, "That he robbed me of my mother."

There is no justice that can be enough because of what I missed out on in life.

*

ANNETTE HANKS
Annette was 39 when she and her husband and their
13-month-old granddaughter were hit by a drunk driver in 2013

I feel our drunk driver got a slap on the wrist and didn't learn a darn thing. At the time of the crash, he was a car salesman and yet he had a suspended license from a prior DUI. A couple of years after the crash, we learned that he was unemployed and a heroin user. Another year later we found out that he was once again selling cars but still had a suspended license.

\*

RENE LEDFORD
Rene's 25-year-old son Justin Colt
was killed by a drunk driver in 2015

At the sentencing hearing, I read a victim's impact statement. I told him that just weeks before the crash, Justin told me that one day I would have to forgive someone for killing him or his sisters. I told my son I never would. He told me, "God forgives you every day. How do you expect him to forgive you if you couldn't forgive someone?"

I told the drunk driver that because of my son's heart and words, that we forgive him, and want him to forgive himself. He was crying, as all of us were too. I know in my heart he is sorry for the choices he made the night he killed my son. He is now in a Texas state prison serving a twelve-year plea agreement.

\*

MELISSA MORIN
Melissa was 30 when she was
hit by a drunk driver in 2013

The driver is a habitual offender. I think people change when *they* are ready to. Within a week or two after the crash he was posting pictures of himself drinking in a bar! He showed no remorse. I don't think the charges were correct: his poor decision took the life of a great woman, mother, and friend. I feel that a DUI offender's license should be revoked instantly, and there should be strict laws for habitual offenders. People make the conscious decision to drink and drive. It ruins, alters, and changes lives forever and yet is one hundred percent preventable. We are forever scarred.

*

LINDA PAULSON
Linda was 40 when her husband and their two
young sons were killed by a drunk driver in 2003

The driver died.

*

NICOLE RAMOS
Nicole was 32 when she and her two
children were hit by a drunk driver in 2013

The driver never faced any legal consequences. I did, however, contact his mother through Facebook to let her know what happened that night, and how he left three adults and four children in the middle of the night while he hid in the country until he decided to knock on someone's door to call for a ride home. I don't know for sure, but I think his mother let him know that she knew because shortly after that, his marriage and family relationships started to fail.

He ended up leaving the state and moving to Colorado, where smoking marijuana is legal. When he got there he continued to party, smoke and drink in excess. After about three months, he met a woman who got him to settle down and become more of a family man. He now regularly posts about how important his kids are and how sorry he is for the pain that he caused his family with his wrongs. I've been praying that he would find his way into the light. Unfortunately, this is still not enough. I would like to be able to tell him all of the things that I had to endure because of his selfish actions, all the pain and mental anguish that my family and I had to go through. I would love to be able to sit down and let him know that there were consequences for what he did, and I paid for it. I would like an apology and a sincere effort to straighten his life out.

*

JEWEL ROSE
Jewel was 39 when she and her family
were hit by a drunk driver in 2012

No, the driver did not face the correct consequences. He was to serve five years if he did not attend counseling sessions while in prison. He did not attend any.

I am beginning to understand why no one shared his court dates with me. I wanted to testify about the lifelong damage this jerk caused my family. I wish I could tell the judge the hell my family has been through. The guy should be serving the full five years, but because I wasn't there, he is now able to kill someone. He did not physically kill any us that day, but we did die in a way. None of us are the same. We are just now starting to see some kind of healing. We are fortunate, yet none of us are safe.

*

LINDSAY WELDON
Lindsay was 21 when she was
hit by a drunk driver in 2012

I feel like he faced the incorrect consequences. If he had faced the correct consequences after the third DUI, he wouldn't have been allowed to have a driver's license. This was his fifth DUI, and he spent five months in jail. I feel that his punishment should've been more severe. The driver is still living in the same city, has the same job, and a new car.

*

RACHAEL WILLIAMS
Rachael was 25 when her 30-year-old husband
Matthew was killed by a drunk driver in 2012

In a perfect world, the driver would die the same way my husband was killed. He wouldn't get free meals in jail and be allowed visitors. He deserves to live in misery, as he is responsible for mine and my children's. He had no remorse; he winked and smiled at me during court dates. He even refused to speak at sentencing. He honestly felt he had done nothing wrong.

In 2016, he became a free man. He has three years of probation remaining. He works a job and just bought a home. I want him to know that he is an evil person. He took away our happiness. He ruined our lives. He took so much away from my daughters. They will never have their dad to walk them down the aisle, attend daddy-daughter dances, or anything else. He took the most important thing from us.

*

# CHAPTER TEN

# POST TRAUMATIC REACTION

Always remember that if you have been diagnosed with PTSD, it is not a sign of weakness. Rather, it is proof of your strength because you have survived.
– MICHEL TEMPLET

Posttraumatic stress is a common reaction caused by a terrifying event. Occurring in people of all ages, it can develop immediately, months or years later. Symptoms include feeling stress or afraid long after the threat is over. Do you suffer from posttraumatic stress as a result of the crash?

\*

JESSICA WEYER BENTLEY
Jessica was 5 when her 24-year-old father
Robert was killed by a drunk driver in 1979

I have posttraumatic stress disorder and suffer mostly from insomnia, flashbacks, and nightmares. Just writing this down for the book caused two nights of insomnia. It is a trigger, revisiting this information. It has lessened with time, but the nightmares are still pretty some days. I talked to a counselor who said I had PTSD. I mainly just spoke to someone when I needed to talk, but I have not received any other kind of treatment.

\*

TIFFANY COLSON
Tiffany was 30 when she was
hit by a drunk driver in 2011

I do not believe that I have any symptoms of posttraumatic stress but my husband says I do. It is hard to drive at night, and it scares me if someone pulls out a little too far. I feel like someone will crash into me for no good reason. It is also very hard to watch any kind of car wreck in movies or online. Even seeing crashes on the news makes me upset.

\*

WENDY DAVIDSON
Wendy was 47 when her 28-year-old son
Chuck was killed by a drunk driver in 2016

I don't feel I've suffered any posttraumatic stress or any other serious issues such as that. I can tell you that my perspective on the world and life has changed dramatically. I can honestly admit that I am no longer the person I was before Chuck died. I've heard that everything happens for a reason, and I used to be a proponent of those words, but it's not that the incident had to happen for a positive, but that a positive resulted from the tragedy.

Sadly, I don't look for these amazing opportunities where I can change the world and make a difference in someone's life, or do something amazing from the outcome of my son's death. I only do what makes me feel better in that instant at this time in my grieving process. I take every possible opportunity to ensure my son's name is spoken and that he is never forgotten.

I can certainly see how events such as these will push people into depression, alcoholism, drug abuse, hoarding, over-shopping and many other excessive things, all in an effort to feel something other than pain. Counseling has helped me, as has reaching out to individuals who are already a part of the club no one wants to join. Now that I'm a new member, it has helped. There is no name for us, no label, but simply parents who have lost children. We don't get a title like widow or orphan, we only get to join a club we didn't want. It's a harsh yet poignant reality.

\*
BILL DOWNS
Bill's 21-year-old son Brad, 19-year-old daughter-in-law
Samantha, and 24-year-old family friend Chris
were killed by a drunk/drugged driver in 2007

I would say, yes. The worst times are around the time of our kids' death, their birthdays, and the holidays.

\*
JULIE DOWNS
Julie's 21-year-old son Brad, 19-year-old daughter-in-law
Samantha, and 24-year-old family friend Chris
were killed by a drunk/drugged driver in 2007

It has been nine years since that tragic night and the things I suffered then are different now. I do have PTSD but it is not as severe as it used to be. At first there were triggers with every breath I took. A sound, a smell, a thought would cause me to envision what the crash must have been like for the kids.

I used to have dreams that I was in the car, and would wake up as Brad's car was impacted by the drunk driver with glass breaking and blood everywhere. The panic attacks I had left me feeling lifeless. The mental pain would become a physical pain like someone had gut-punched me. I would curl up in a fetal position and beg God to take me because I could not endure it any longer.

Nothing I did would or could control the pain I felt. I tried medication and I tried coping skills that my grief counselor taught me, but I found that time was the only thing that helped. I learned not to fight the feelings that I was feeling but to embrace them, and they would pass. Time eased the intensity of the pain. Now, nine years later, I still have panic attacks that bring me to tears, but they do not last as long and I bounce back from them more quickly. They are not as frequent nor as intense, and I have learned to manage them.

*

MICHAEL GERSHE<br>
Michael was 8-weeks-old when his 28-year-old<br>
mother Barbara was killed by a drunk driver in 1970

I am sure a therapist would say I suffer from PTSD in some form, even though I was an infant at the time of the crash. I don't have to recall the crash to have that stress in my life. I never sought treatment to specifically talk about the crash, but I have met with a therapist to discuss my best friend's death. A few years ago I did talk to a rabbi when I was struggling with questions for which there are no answers.

When it was time to get my driver's license, I wondered if I could drive a car knowing that a car crash changed my life. Granted, it wasn't the car but a drunk driver who hit our car, yet I doubted myself about my ability to drive. Even today, with so many distracted drivers on the road, I get a bit nervous because I just don't want to be in another crash. Not nervous to the point that I am a bad driver, but nervous enough to be more observant of other people.

I don't like being out on holidays either, because drunk drivers ruin it for everyone. The older I get, the more I want to be a hermit, but if I do that then I feel the drunk driver wins. I know the dangers out there on the roads, and it still scares me.

I also tend to get emotional whiles watching shows where something happens that tragically impacts a parent. For example, I was watching *The Flash* and when he went back in time to save his mother, I started to cry. It's those type of things that are a challenge to deal with. I wish I had the power to get one chance to talk with my mother.

*

ANNETTE HANKS
Annette was 39 when she and her husband and their
13-month-old granddaughter were hit by a drunk driver in 2013

PTSD has affected me greatly. As I write this, it's been three and a half years since the crash and I still wake up screaming from nightmares. I have serious issues being a passenger in a car, and there are times when I can't be in a car at all. I've taken all my pain and hurt and used it as fuel to fight impaired driving. I am a peer supporter and victim advocate with MADD, and help other victims and survivors of DUI crashes. This has helped me in my healing process.

*

RENE LEDFORD
Rene's 25-year-old son Justin Colt
was killed by a drunk driver in 2015

We all have our okay days, and then there are the days that consume us in the emptiness of not having Justin Colt. We feel his presence daily, with all the signs he sends us. His love will forever be with us, and we feel so blessed to have gotten twenty-five years one month and six days to have him in our physical lives.

The emptiness is the most engulfing for me. I miss running my hand through his hair, I miss our talks, his hugs, his "I love you, Mom," his tender heart, his beautiful smile and smirky laugh. I miss our moments. I miss HIM.

\*

MELISSA MORIN
Melissa was 30 when she was
hit by a drunk driver in 2013

I do suffer from PTSD. I tried medication but I don't like prescription drugs, period. The anxiety and panic attacks are the worst. I had flashbacks for a long time but that has lessened and nearly stopped, though it was horrible the first year. I just felt like if I talked to a psychologist, it was no different than telling a friend. Regardless of what anyone had to say, it wasn't going to make me feel any different. It literally took time for me to heal mentally and emotionally.

\*

LINDA PAULSON
Linda was 40 when her husband and their two
young sons were killed by a drunk driver in 2003

Yes, I suffer from posttraumatic stress. My treatment is medicine for PTSD, depression, and anxiety. My PTSD has stayed the same.

\*

NICOLE RAMOS
Nicole was 32 when she and her two
children were hit by a drunk driver in 2013

When my case was dropped, I lost it. I sought help by reaching out to MADD and they put me in touch with a crime victim advocate and counseling. I was having nightmares, anxiety, and depression about my physical limitations and dependency on others. My daughter, who was thirteen at the time, and I went to four sessions to be able to talk through what all went down that night and our fears for our future. Over time, my nightmares decreased, anxiety became less frequent, and my rage started to turn into action for change. Now I might have episodes of frustration of my physical limitations and fear about getting into another wreck, but mostly I deal with this by talking to people close to me. I no longer seek counseling or take medication.

*

JEWEL ROSE
Jewel was 39 when she and her family
were hit by a drunk driver in 2012

At first, I had debilitating flashbacks. I could not think, or speak at all. My sentences came out garbled when I was stressed. One of the school counselors, with whom I have a good relationship, has noted how different I am today compared to then. Only her perspective was of the injured me, I was in no condition to fight for my kids, but I had no choice.

Thankfully, a good attorney found a great forensic neuropsychologist who helped me. She diagnosed my symptoms and that was the first step to recovery. It is possible, yet pills and talk therapy go only so far. I went to Cerebrum Health Care Centers in Texas to really get the help I needed. No pill could have helped as much as the exercises they gave me. They got to the root of my fatigue and fully supported the therapy for the trauma, which I needed. I was able to sleep after three years. Only then was my brain able to begin the true healing process.

*

LINDSAY WELDON
Lindsay was 21-years-old when she
was hit by a drunk driver in 2012

Yes, I suffer from PTSD as a result. No one symptom is the most challenging. Every symptom is a challenge. I've gone to doctors, specialists, and therapists. Treatment right now consists of numerous medications, and I'm still working with a psychiatrist to get my medications just right. PTSD doesn't consist of just one thing or symptom, there are many, and for multiple different symptoms, there is a need for different medications. I'm currently taking seven medications for nightmares, anxiety, depression, balanced moods, and sleep. I'm maxed out on the dosages so they've also prescribed booster medications that go hand in hand so I get the help I need.

\*

RACHAEL WILLIAMS
Rachael was 25 when her 30-year-old husband
Matthew was killed by a drunk driver in 2012

Although I wasn't present for the accident, I've been diagnosed with PTSD and depression. I attend counseling once a week and I am on medications to help cope. I tried for three years to do it on my own, and I needed help.

\*

SHELLY WOODWARD
Shelly was 30 when her 16-month old son was injured in a
drunk driving crash caused by Shelly's former husband in 1996

I did suffer from the loss of my material possessions and my marriage. I was in an emotional grief period and mad at myself for allowing this to happen. That was my thought process at the time. Now I know there was nothing I could have done. I should have never married him, I should have left him after he hit me the first time after drinking. My heart hoped that maybe when he saw the love I had to give, he would change. This wasn't the case. He is an alcoholic, and only he could change that.

My therapy was becoming a speaker for MADD in Ohio and South Carolina. It helped me to talk about it, to tell my story, to let people see that it does happen. It was not my fault, it was not my son's fault. My ex-husband did this, not us.

I am still angry because he is still drinking. He has never been a father to my son. He has never been there for him, emotionally or physically. I feel bad for my son. Even though he has a lot of friends and family who love him, we are not his father. He was too little to remember the crash, but he saw the person his father was while growing up. If his father would have changed, the relationship would have also. My son tells people he doesn't have a father, and to me that's sad, but understandable.

*

By holding onto unforgiveness, I became
a prisoner of my own bitterness, hate and
anger. Releasing those things and forgiving
the drunk driver has set me free.

JULIE DOWNS

*

# CHAPTER ELEVEN

# IMPACT ON RELATIONSHIPS

Friendship isn't about who you've known the longest. It's about who walked into your life and said, "I'm here for you," and proved it. -UNKNOWN

When something tragic happens, we crave social connection. It is our human nature. Support from friends and familial relationships are critical to our ability to develop resilience after a disaster. But relationships can be tested during times of great stress. In the face of tragedy, some relationships remain steady as a rock, and even strengthened while others dissolve. Did the crash impact any of your relationships?

\*

JESSICA WEYER BENTLEY
Jessica was 5 when her 24-year-old father
Robert was killed by a drunk driver in 1979

When a loved one is lost, it goes beyond that loss and impacts all who knew and loved the individual. When Dad was killed, it severed an entire side of family from me. My dad's family was all but lost to me as I grew up in a different state, away from his family. I lost an entire half of who I am. Recently, we have all connected on social media and share stories and pictures. When a loved one dies, they take a huge part of us with them.

\*

SHANNON BOOS
Shannon was 20 when her 21-year-old brother
Kevin was killed by a drunk driver in 2015

All of my relationships have been changed in one way or another. Some were tainted with change, others completely shattered. However, in the darkness of the loss of Kevin, some relationships have actually flourished.

Before Kevin died, my relationships with my cousins and maternal aunts and uncles had been on the rocks. We weren't really talking, and time spent together was filled with awkward tension. In hindsight, I honestly don't remember much of why it was like this, other than we had been in a rough patch of our relationships. When Kevin died, all this changed. And if I have to pick something that I am grateful for (even though I don't like using the term "grateful" when it comes to Kevin's death), it would be how strong my relationships with my cousins, aunts, and uncles have become. We are closer than ever, and I find strength and comfort through their love and hugs.

In my opinion, that's how it should be. Any death, especially that of a sudden, traumatic death of a young person like Kevin, should bring people, especially family, together. It should show how the trivial things in life just don't matter. We should love each other and laugh together every single day. Because life is so short and oh, so fragile. However, this isn't always the case.

So many relationships in my life have changed dramatically since Kevin was killed, and these changes have easily had some of the most powerful impacts on me in the past year. So many people I called best friends I haven't heard from in months. I'm sure that when confronted, there'll be many excuses. Their life has continued and they expect mine to as well. I've heard every excuse in the book.

"Sorry, I was busy today." They still have time to post social media pictures and updates, but can't send a quick text message.

"Your grief makes me uncomfortable." My grief makes *you* uncomfortable? I'm so sorry that the immense pain I feel is too much for you to handle. Next.

"I thought it would be better for you if I left your life." I'm sorry, what?

When I think of the relationships that have been affected, two people come to mind first. These two people were like a second set of parents to me for quite some time, and I even came to love their son who was a baby at the time, more than anything in the world. We had a falling out before Kevin was killed, but I still reached out to them when he died because they had offered a sense of comfort for so long. They were incredibly supportive for the first few days. They came to the funeral, called to check on me, etc. But then their world kept going, and mine was expected to continue turning too. Their true colors were always right in front to see, but I really didn't have a clear view until my phone calls and text messages went unanswered two weeks after my brother's funeral.

I have finally learned to accept that anyone who is a true friend would not have an excuse. Sadly, now I can count my true friends on only one hand.

This is how it happens. Your loved one dies. There's a funeral. Hundreds of people show up to offer hugs and condolences. You start to think, wow, maybe I can do this. Maybe I can get through this. These people surround you with so much love and support that it makes all the scary, heartbreaking parts of death blurry. But in reality, these people go to a funeral and then go home. That's it. Time to get on with their lives. They don't have time for you or your pain. They expect you to just pick up and keep moving. In some cases this might be possible, like when it's an older loved one who is sick and dying. Of course it hurts when they pass, but some feel relief that their loved one is now "in a better place."

But when your twenty-one-year-old brother and two of his best friends are killed by a drunk driver, and people try to tell you that he's in a better place, it's a smack in the face.

He's in a better place? Where? Can I go? Because I'm pretty sure there is no better place than here, with our family and me.

He wasn't sick. He wasn't in pain. He was killed. Murdered. Gone in a second.

There are also friends who don't understand why you haven't moved on. Frankly, it has been over a year and I still haven't moved on. I still cry about Kevin. Mostly in private, but I still do.

I remember one moment in particular. A friend had come to me for advice. It hadn't even been a month since Kevin was killed, and she was looking for a shoulder to cry on because of some sort of boy issues she was having. I politely explained that I was in no place to offer advice or comfort because I was still lacking relief for my own pain. This started a huge argument that ended with my friend calling me selfish for not helping her with her problems. But I was too caught up in my own. This friend was, in effect, asking me to help her with her stubbed toe, while I was trying to cope with missing half my body.

To this day, I still struggle to understand the logic and thought that went into the words and actions (or lack of them) from friends and even some of my family. If someone I loved had lost someone so traumatically, I would do anything and everything I could to be there and help. If I wasn't sure what to do, I would ask. I try to give the benefit of the doubt because I've never been on that side.

I don't hear from a lot of my old friends anymore. And I guess that's okay because I've narrowed down my group of friends to those who truly care and want to help me through this horrible, horrible "journey." At the end of the day, I learned a lot about these people. They weren't ever really my friends. Anyone who truly loves and cares about me would be there, no questions asked, no excuses. Some were, and still are, and I am so grateful for them.

If I could offer any sort of advice to a friend of a bereaved person who is be reading this, it would be this: speak up. Talk to your friend. Ask how they are. Talk about their loved one(s). Ask about them. Tell stories about them. Because I promise you, the amount of discomfort you feel about the situation doesn't compare to the amount of pain your friend is feeling. And he or she hasn't moved on, hasn't forgotten.

It astounds me how quiet my phone has gotten over the past year, especially on holidays and Kevin's birthday and anniversaries of his death. I think that people assume that my family and I have moved on, or we don't want to hear from anyone. But they are so wrong. I've even called people out on this, whether privately or on a rant on social media. But there are still people who refuse to speak up. And I will never, ever understand that.

*

TIFFANY COLSON<br>Tiffany was 30 when she was<br>hit by a drunk driver in 2011

There wasn't one relationship that was impacted more than others. They all were. This wreck caused some people to leave my life, which is good because I do not need any negativity in my life. It did strengthen my marriage. My depression caused me to never feel loved by anyone. After the wreck, I saw that my husband was there for me no matter what. He showed me what "in health and in sickness" really meant.

\*

WENDY DAVIDSON
Wendy was 47 when her 28-year-old son
Chuck was killed by a drunk driver in 2016

Family support? Family relationships? I'm not sure where to begin. There were individuals in my family who told me Chuck was in a better place and that he wasn't suffering. Suffering? He was twenty-eight years old, finishing college, on his own, making his way in the world. He wasn't suffering here, and his place was with his family, period.

I had members of my family argue the semantics of the definition of murder. The driver who killed my son is a murderer, period. I had family abandon me when I needed them the most because they were uncomfortable around certain people. There were topics so unrelated to his death that were brought up the day after he died, such as money owed. I had a member of my family try to convince my youngest daughter that she would be better living her life four states away. The selfish and senseless ideas and notions people get in their head that they think will "help" the bereaved is mind boggling.

If you are ever in a horrible situation where a family member or friend has lost a child, my advice is to simply be present. Don't disappear, but don't try to fix the unfixable either. You don't have to do or say anything, just be present in their life. Never say "They are in a better place," or start a sentence with "At least…" It's *not* helpful. The best thing to say is "I'm sorry," and "I'm here for you if you need me." It speaks volumes; it did for me at least.

It was the individuals in my life who were just present who helped me the most. Some relationships in my family are now broken after my son's death, some have improved. I don't really care, I just miss my son, and ache for my living children who still suffer. Although he isn't Chuck's father, I'm grateful for my husband. He has been by my side through all of this and if it weren't for him, I'm not sure where I'd be.

*

BILL DOWNS
Bill's 21-year-old son Brad, 19-year-old daughter-in-law
Samantha, and 24-year-old family friend Chris
were killed by a drunk/drugged driver in 2007

Our daughter is mentally handicapped, and has been affected by the kids' death more than we realized. She often talks to them and even argues with them at times. Special people sense things in a different way than we do.

I guess the one relationship that was affected most by the kids' death was our marriage. The anger and hate I harbored inside the first four months after the kids' death was very hard on our marriage. My wife in constant prayer was the only thing that kept our marriage from falling apart. Today our love is stronger than ever before and though we miss the kids desperately, their death has strengthened our marriage so we can help others through this nightmare.

*

JULIE DOWNS
Julie's 21-year-old son Brad, 19-year-old daughter-in-law
Samantha, and 24-year-old family friend Chris
were killed by a drunk/drugged driver in 2007

At the time of the kids' death I had been happily married for twenty-five years. Bill and I were very close and I was confident that nothing could shake the foundation that our love was built on, but that confidence was shattered as they lowered my son into the grave. I became a scared, frightened, fragile individual, and in a sense I became very selfish. I knew Bill was hurting, but I couldn't do anything to help him because my pain was so great. I was Brad's *mother*. I carried Brad in *my body* and held him in *my arms* as I fed him from *my breast*. Brad was *my baby*. In my pain, I saw my loss as greater than anyone else's, even greater than Bill's.

I was the one who needed support. I needed Bill to comfort me. I could not focus on his pain and what he was feeling, because I couldn't even deal with my own pain. I tried to be there for him, but it always turned into what I was going through. I didn't see what I was doing, but in my trying to survive the death of my son I was slowly pushing Bill away. I would feel such guilt finding comfort in Bill's arms. I deserved to feel nothing but sadness and pain; after all, Brad was *my child*. How could I be comforted?

I moved out of our bed because I couldn't sleep at night. I sat outside on the deck or slept sitting in a recliner. In doing so I moved farther away from Bill. On occasion, when we did try to make love, I would pull away, crying. How could I feel such emotion when my child was dead? I was buried with Brad, Sam and Chris. I didn't know how to crawl out of that grave.

Bill and I stumbled through the next couple of years. Time has a way of going on even though you are stuck in your pain. I didn't realize that our marriage and relationship was suffering. We both had gotten so good at faking our feelings that we just saw the distance that had grown between us as part of our new reality. I loved Bill and I took him for granted. I didn't understand or see what he was going through. I was so wrapped up in my own feelings, and I just assumed he was dealing with his grief in the same way I was dealing with mine. I had turned to God to find comfort and I was breathing again, but Bill wasn't. He wasn't dealing with his feelings; he was ignoring them, and his anger was consuming him. I didn't know he was keeping everything bottled up inside because I was expressing enough feelings for the both of us. Focusing only on what I had lost, I didn't see what he had lost, and because of this our marriage was dying.

On October 21, 2011, I planned a fiftieth birthday celebration for Bill. I bought him a cake and ice cream and even a gift. This was the first birthday we had acknowledged since the kids' death, and I was feeling pretty good about it but Bill rejected everything I had done. His actions and words cut through my heart like a knife. He was so angry at me that I just went into the bedroom and lay across the bed and cried. The next day we had church, and Bill still seemed to be angry. I apologized to him and he just brushed it off. He didn't want to talk about it. During church for the first time in twenty-nine years he placed his Bible between us so we were not sitting side by side, and not once did he hold my hand or put his arm around me like he had done so many times before. I was heartbroken and confused.

When we got out to the car for our ride home, I asked him what was wrong. He looked straight ahead without answering, so I became more persistent.

I asked again, and finally his answer to me was "*I don't love you anymore!*"

My heart fell out of my chest. How could that be?

My first reaction was to turn to our pastor for help. He talked with us together and talked with Bill separately, but Bill stayed steadfast. He had fallen out of love with me and he hated everything, especially life and himself. He wanted nothing to do with me nor with God, and he just wanted to be left alone. I tried talking to him, but his replies sliced me in half. He would say that he cared for me only because I was the mother of his children, but that was as deep as his feelings went. He said he also realized that he had never loved me at all.

I started sleeping back in bed just to be a presence there, hoping that he would feel my love for him. I would reach over every night and, with the tip of my finger, I would write "I love you" on his chest. He wouldn't pull away or respond; he would just lie there. He had told me that he didn't want me to verbalize my love, and when I did try he would just ignore what I said. I was so confused and hurt. He did not want to sleep in the spare bedroom, nor did he want a divorce. He just wanted me to leave him alone. I was lost and did not know what to do except pray. I prayed morning, noon and night for over a year. I begged God to enter Bill's heart because I knew that if Bill would open his heart to God, he would also let me back in.

I read every book I could on marriage and why men fall out of love, searching for an answer on how to save my marriage, but Bill slipped farther away. I didn't know from one day to the next if he would walk out on me and our daughter, or if he would stay. He would throw me enough crumbs to give me hope that maybe he did love me, only to be nasty to me all over again.

I continued to pray. I started leaning more on God, knowing that whatever happened, Cindy and I would be okay. I stopped begging Bill to love me and started not caring. But I still prayed. My feelings were hardening toward what Bill was doing to me, and I was feeling stronger. I would never give him a divorce because I did not believe in divorce, but I was not against separation.

After one year and two months, Bill's disrespect was more than I could handle. I did not deserve to be treated the way he was treating me, and although I was tired of praying, I still prayed.

On December 6, 2012, we got into an argument and I told him to leave. I was finished. I was no longer going to be a doormat for him, so I kicked him out. He left and was gone for an hour, and then I heard him pull back into the driveway. I put a pillow and blanket on the couch and locked myself in the bedroom. He knocked on the bedroom door and I ignored him. He stood there for a moment and I heard him walk away. I cried myself to sleep that night, praying. Not only had I lost my son, but also my husband and marriage.

I woke up at 4 a.m. and went into the living room. I sat on the couch next to Bill and just looked at him. How had we gotten to this point? He was sleeping but sensed that someone was there, and opened his eyes. He stared at me with tears running down his cheeks and begged me to forgive him. I told him that the only way we could go forward was if he agreed to counseling. He said, "Call the counselor and make an appointment!"

On our first visit, the counselor listened to Bill talk. She then looked at him and said, "Bill, you are a walking dead person." Bill started crying because that was exactly how he felt. The counselor said she couldn't help us with our marriage problem until Bill properly grieved his son. So together we worked through Bill losing Brad, and then our love for each other that was clouded by the pain resurfaced and we were able to save our marriage. On February 9, 2013, during church service, Bill and I both rededicated our lives to the Lord and Bill was rebaptized. That night, in front of family and friends, we renewed our vows. My prayers were answered. Marriages can survive a tragedy.

*

MICHAEL GERSHE
Michael was 8-weeks-old when his 28-year-old
mother Barbara was killed by a drunk driver in 1970

. I know the crash impacted my father's relationship with my mother's family. I recall hanging out with my maternal cousins a few times as a kid, but we don't have a relationship now as adults. We've exchanged a few emails here and there over the years, but really we haven't kept in touch. I do stay in contact with my aunt though, and she has given me pictures of my mom from childhood which are pretty precious to me.

I don't want to say my relationship with my father is strained, because it's not. But I always wanted him to talk more about the crash and about my mother while I was growing up. I was always scared to talk to him about it because I didn't want to bring up those painful memories for him. But I wanted him to open up about it to me and my brother without us prodding, if you know what I mean.

I think when I date someone, I keep a wall up so that person does not see all the pain inside. I deflect most things with humor. I am sure that drives her crazy, but it is a defense mechanism. There are times where I will withdraw from a person, not because of what they have done, but because I am going through a depressed state. I don't like asking for help and I tend to internalize my pain, because it's mine and don't want to put it upon someone else. But that has caused some issues in relationships, and I have to do better otherwise I will end up alone if I keep that wall up all the time. It's weird, I can open up my soul on stage or in this book for instance, but sitting across from someone who has feelings for me and vice versa and sharing those same thoughts is tough. What can I say? I'm a tortured soul!

*

ANNETTE HANKS
Annette was 39 when she and her husband and their
13-month-old granddaughter were hit by a drunk driver in 2013

We are blessed in the fact that the trauma brought our family closer. My husband and I suffered the same trauma so we can relate and we discuss it and check up on each other. If one of us is having a hard day because of memories of the crash, we sit and talk about our granddaughter and how silly and beautiful she is. She is the light of our lives.

\*

RENE LEDFORD
Rene's 25-year-old son Justin Colt
was killed by a drunk driver in 2015

Death brings out the truth in people. There are a couple members of my family who hurt my parents, daughters and myself by their actions and words in the week after the crash and funeral. We have forgiven but still remember their actions and words. We have come to realize that until it happens to them as an individual, they will never understand our pain. We have chosen to only discuss certain things with certain people due to how private Justin Colt was. There are the ones who don't stop to think before they speak, and that's when I wish people and family would just say nothing at all. Justin Colt is my son. My daughters, my parents and myself are his voice now. No one knows the true pain unless you have lost a child. No parent under any circumstances should ever bury their child, and some people will never know until it happens to them, how harsh, uncompassionate, cruel, unspeakable actions and words can destroy someone after this kind of loss.

\*

MELISSA MORIN
Melissa was 30 when she was
hit by a drunk driver in 2013

It caused a strain in my relationship with my fiancé. We made it through the hardest part of facing the injuries and surgeries. For me, I knew he was my everything. He took care of me, even bathed and wiped me because I couldn't do it myself. To be in a position to be unable to do simple things for yourself is embarrassing. Obviously I couldn't help myself, literally, and he did it with no hesitation. I don't think either of us knew what the emotion and trauma would do not just to me, but I think both of us. It definitely changed me, everything we've been through. I know he understands but also gets frustrated from all of the physical challenges and my crazy emotions, but at the end of the day, I do believe our love is still very strong. As time goes by, its gets better. I don't believe that there is a time limit on healing. It's been almost three years. My scars definitely make me feel insecure.

*

LINDA PAULSON
Linda was 40 when her husband and their two
young sons were killed by a drunk driver in 2003

None of my relationships were really impacted.

*

NICOLE RAMOS
Nicole was 32 when she and her two
children were hit by a drunk driver in 2013

Before the crash, my mother and brother were in a feud. I was in the neutral zone and trying to help them work it out. My mother also had a vacation planned with my aunt to Costa Rica that they won on a game show. Because I needed constant care, my mother had to move in with me. She left her home, husband, and pets in California for over six months to become my full-time caretaker. I remember my older brother FaceTiming me around my birthday, about a month and a half after the crash, and when he realized my mom was there taking care of me, all communication stopped. I texted him and called him, with no response. I assumed that he was upset with me or our mother. I went California for the summer and went to his house to visit. He never even came out of his room, his wife said he was not feeling well. He never called to invite us over, and that's when I knew that things were strained. My aunt and mother were unable to reschedule their trip so my aunt went without her, and took a friend in her place. This also caused some strife in their relationship, so I called my aunt apologizing because I felt that it was my fault that she could not go, which caused them to argue. The relationships between my mother, aunt and brother were all complicated because of the time and commitment my mother made to care for me.

*

JEWEL ROSE<br>Jewel was 39 when she and her family<br>were hit by a drunk driver in 2012

There is no way to identify which one. When everything about you changes, so do your relationships. Since I used to run every day, my daily life changed. Now, I can't because of extreme pain in my neck and lower back. The headaches are too intense after my run, which keeps me from working. I don't run so that I can work. Basic need met, yet at a huge price. The relationship with my self-confidence has suffered most. I am no longer confident enough to play any game for fear that my mouth and brain won't work together. I remember how agile and athletic I was, and I have to keep the basics of life going before I can conquer this fear. I will conquer it, but for now I need to focus on my husband, my kids and keeping our bills paid.

The relationship between my husband and I has suffered a great deal because he had to be superman. He just didn't have "Super S" on his shirt. He paid the bills, cleaned the house, and managed our medical bills, which is no small feat for a family of four all needing medical care. He did this while my kids were being targeted by the school system, my father was dying of cancer, and while he was an amazing Scout master! He shouldered many burdens and I know he resented it. We are healing through this now. Thankfully, he has stayed with me when I needed him most.

As for my kids, they resented my care for them, stating I was over protective. In this world, the "get back into the ball game" mentality takes precedence. Keep in mind, I put myself through college on scholarships, played four sports in school and club volleyball. Plus, I rowed on the Washington State crew team. I know that mantra and believed it. I still do, it just looks different.

Only recently have my kids been able to see the care in my actions. Our relationship was shattered but is now healing. Love does conquer all, but it also takes time.

*

LINDSAY WELDON
Lindsay was 21 when she was
hit by a drunk driver in 2012

I would say that the relationship that has been impacted the most is mine and my husband's. PTSD and all its symptoms are hard for me, and even harder for my husband. He doesn't always know what to do or say to help me. He does his best though.

*

RACHAEL WILLIAMS
Rachael was 25 when her 30-year-old husband
Matthew was killed by a drunk driver in 2012

I lost a lot of relationships with friends and family because they didn't understand what I was going through. I used to be close with my mom and dad and now, not so much. We stick to ourselves because that way no one can hurt us.

*

SHELLY WOODWARD
Shelly was 30 when her 16-month old son was injured in a
drunk driving crash caused by Shelly's former husband in 1996

My older two daughters don't drink and drive, not even once. They have always called me, even if it's 2 a.m. I am grateful for that. My son is empty. He wants a dad, a father — he wants his dad. That will never happen. I have never stood in the way of his relationship with his father. I merely provided the safety of not allowing him in the car for visits with his father.

His father remarried several years ago, and at first his wife was kind and I felt this relationship would be a good influence on my son's father. That was not to be. They went through a very personal death in the family and she mentally fell apart. She began to hate my son and me. It was very hard to maintain any relationship between my son and his father. She didn't want my son around, and it showed. My son has dealt with so much emotionally, and I can understand why he has spent years in therapy trying to work through everything.

*

I've gotten some really great advice from
people these past few months, and one
piece of advice in particular: I will survive this.

WENDY DAVIDSON

*

CHAPTER TWELVE

# TESTING THE FAITH

Love is the only law capable of transforming grief
into hope. -LYNDA CHELDELIN FELL

Tragedies can have far-reaching effects in many areas of our life, including faith. For some, faith deepens as it becomes a safe haven for sorrow. For others, it becomes a source of disappointment leading to fractured beliefs. Has your faith been affected by the crash and, if so, how?

\*

JESSICA WEYER BENTLEY
Jessica was 5 when her 24-year-old father
Robert was killed by a drunk driver in 1979

My faith is stronger. I feel God lies close to me. It's comforting knowing that God loves me, and I, him. When shaken to your core, you feel faith in a different way.

\*

SHANNON BOOS
Shannon was 20 when her 21-year-old brother
Kevin was killed by a drunk driver in 2015

I was raised in a Catholic home because my mother has always been very religious. My father, not so much. Nonetheless, my brothers and I were taken to church every Sunday. As I got older, I started to drift away from religion for many reasons. Whenever something painful happened, one of my first thoughts would be if there is a God, why do things like this happen?

When Kevin was killed, this question still popped into my head. I cannot think of any reason why God would take my brother and our two friends like that, to be killed in such a senseless way, so quickly and so traumatically.

I have always tried to believe that everything happens for a reason. In some cases, I do believe it is true. For instance, when I was in high school my dream college was the University of Florida. But even after all my hard work, I was rejected by the school. I was absolutely devastated. I attended my second choice school, Florida State University, for two years with Kevin and my two friends Morgan and Cenzo by my side. If I had been accepted into UF, I wouldn't have had those two amazing years with three angels, so that is something I believe happened for a reason. However, there is absolutely no reason the three of them had to be killed. If you try to feed me this, I won't believe you. I don't know if there is a God. But if there is, I don't ever want to know him.

*

TIFFANY COLSON<br>Tiffany was 30 when she was<br>hit by a drunk driver in 2011

I was not raised in a religious family so there were no questions about my faith. I am more of a spiritual person. I do not know all the answers so I will not say that there isn't a god. I just choose to believe more in being a good person, positive energy, and karma. What you send out into the world will come back to you, whether it is good or bad. I also had to look at the wreck in a different way. This wasn't a punishment for me, it was a lesson for the drunk driver. He lost his wife and kids.

\*

WENDY DAVIDSON
Wendy was 47 when her 28-year-old son
Chuck was killed by a drunk driver in 2016

I'm an extremely spiritual person, but not in a biblical sense. I've studied many religions and what they offer and teach are certainly worth paying attention to, and striving to live by and emulate. I do not subscribe to any religion, I don't go to church, I don't pray, and I don't hate anything. I refuse to tell myself anything contrary to what I believe because it's not what I believed before Chuck's death, and it shouldn't change after.

I help people when I can. I will give my last dollar if someone needs it more than me, I will offer my home to whoever needs a roof, food to anyone who is hungry, and my time if it's called upon or needed. I don't treat my body badly, and I don't live recklessly. Aren't all those things spiritual in themselves? Aren't they things that all religions practice and preach to live by? I have faith in myself and my family because I can touch, see, and smell them.

No one will ever know what it is like to die. No one will ever know where you go when you die. It's a question that can never be answered until you are dead, so I make no pretenses on what could or should be beyond death. My reality is that my son is dead and right now he is no longer with me.

\*

BILL DOWNS
Bill's 21-year-old son Brad, 19-year-old daughter-in-law
Samantha, and 24-year-old family friend Chris
were killed by a drunk/drugged driver in 2007

Ever since I was thirteen when I gave my life to Christ the first time, I felt I could handle anything. I thought my faith in God was very strong and there was nothing I would face that I could not handle. When our kids were killed, my faith was all but destroyed. My wife and marriage faced a challenge we had never experienced. Her constant prayers and faith is the only thing that kept our marriage from failing.

*

JULIE DOWNS

Julie's 21-year-old son Brad, 19-year-old daughter-in-law<br>Samantha, and 24-year-old family friend Chris<br>were killed by a drunk/drugged driver in 2007

When everything is going great in life we tend to praise God, but when everything falls apart, it is so easy to blame Him. Especially when your relationship with Him is not what you thought it was. Before the crash, God was who I wanted Him to be. He fit into my life and accepted me on my terms. I considered myself a Christian. I had accepted Jesus as my savior and I had been baptized. I went to church when I wanted to and I read my Bible on occasion. I prayed when I had a need and thanked Him because my prayers were answered. Life was good. I had a wonderful husband and two beautiful kids. We lived in a nice house and always had food on the table. We were all healthy and safe. We lived a happy life and we were good people. I never dreamed that tragedy could touch our lives, and when it did, I was not prepared for it.

Was I such a bad person that God would punish me in this way? I shook my fist at heaven and asked Him "Why?" If God truly loved me, then why did He let my kids die? I had said my prayers that day asking for God's protection over my family. Did He not hear me? I even questioned if there truly was a God. I struggled with my lack of faith for nearly two years. I tried to pray but couldn't, because I didn't know if He truly heard my prayers. I would turn the radio on during the day to hear something besides silence and listen to Christian music that I would angrily turn off because it would speak to my heart. God never left me as I was struggling to find Him. I was living in a fog and couldn't see Him through the pain. But He never gave up on me. I found Him one day in a song. The words to the song touched my heart and I realized that God did not kill my son, the drunk driver did. I opened my heart to God's comfort, and He eagerly came in.

He doesn't promise that bad things won't happen, but He does promise to be there to comfort us when it does. Now, my relationship with God is not on my terms, it's on His terms. He is God and He will never change, and I have chosen to trust Him no matter what. God will not force Himself on us. He has given us free will to choose. Sometimes that freewill gets us into trouble, like it did that tragic night when the drunk driver used her free will to make the choice to drink and drive.

Without my newfound faith, I wouldn't be able to face tomorrow. My hope is in Christ. I know that one day I will see my kids again, because He promised. I will be able to ask why this tragedy happened, but I know that the reason will no longer matter because I will be with my Savior and reunited with my son.

*

MICHAEL GERSHE
Michael was 8-weeks-old when his 28-year-old
mother Barbara was killed by a drunk driver in 1970

I have definitely questioned God many, many times during my life. Questioned Him, cursed Him, and questioned Him even more. I was raised Jewish, but even though I had my Bar Mitzvah, I don't really practice the faith like I should. I mean, I even eat bacon, so that should tell you something. However, I'd like to think that I adhere to Jewish principals in my life, which to me is better than going to Temple. Of course, any rabbi would disagree and would want me there.

I was angry with God a lot during college because that is when I was really thinking about my own existence. I wondered why He killed my mother at a young age but kept me alive. Why did He spare my life when I was only an infant? Why did He have to be so cruel and take her from my, our family? I hated Him for a long time and stayed mad at God for it. I believed the anger was justified. However, He had a purpose for me, which turned out to be true because eventually I created The Magic of Life program which has allowed me to make a difference.

A few years ago, my anger toward God returned, and I had a lot of questions for Him. I am not even sure the catalyst for it this time around, but something set me off. I contacted a local rabbi and met with him about it and, after a nice discussion, he told me to read the book, "Why Bad Things Happen To Good People," by Harold Kushner. The book did help, but I am not sure if it restored my faith. I try to be a good son that my mother would be proud of, which, to me, is more important than satisfying the man upstairs. Since I cannot get the answers I seek from God, I just have to try to live a good life the best I can. It makes me angry at times, but staying mad does no good and is not healthy. I just have to believe that my mother's purpose was to give me life, and I cannot let her death be for nothing. My purpose was to create my program, share my story, and keep my mother's legacy alive.

*

ANNETTE HANKS
Annette was 39 when she and her husband and their
13-month-old granddaughter were hit by a drunk driver in 2013

We saw God's hands working from the very start. A friend from church just happened to be driving by and stopped at the crash site. When I was at the hospital waiting for the ambulance carrying Adilyn, another friend from church showed up at the hospital for her appointment. We know God placed them there for comfort for us. And God placed a police officer across the street moments before the crash. He was at the scene in seconds. That officer is now a very special part of our family.

We believe that God saved our granddaughter because He has a great purpose for her life. She is four years old now and she is amazing. From the minute she woke up at Harborview Medical Center, she amazed all the doctors. She saw three specialists at Seattle Children's Hospital for multiple follow-up visits, and every single time they said that absolutely nothing was wrong with her and that they didn't understand how that could be, given all the injuries she sustained. This precious baby girl had the biggest, darkest, ugliest, swollen black eye for six months, but she always had a smile on her face. We know God is the ultimate healer!

*

RENE LEDFORD
Rene's 25-year-old son Justin Colt
was killed by a drunk driver in 2015

As Justin Colts mom, my faith has grown stronger. My youngest daughter, her faith comes and goes. My oldest daughter doesn't understand why Justin Colt was killed. She doesn't have much faith. Her beliefs are her own and I don't push her. I pray for understanding and guidance for us all.

*

MELISSA MORIN
Melissa was 30 when she was
hit by a drunk driver in 2013

I couldn't have gotten through all of this without the power of prayer. I literally prayed every day. Naturally one definitely asks why, but at the end of the day, nothing you do can change the situation. All you can do is roll with the punches. My faith is definitely stronger.

\*

LINDA PAULSON
Linda was 40 when her husband and their two
young sons were killed by a drunk driver in 2003

The crash has made my faith a lot stronger.

\*

NICOLE RAMOS
Nicole was 32 when she and her two
children were hit by a drunk driver in 2013

My faith never wavered. In fact, when the dust and smoke started to settle as our vehicle came to rest on the side of the road, I thanked God for the sounds of my kids screaming in the backseat. That meant that they had survived an impact that I assumed killed us immediately. Days later when I looked back at the fact that I was never in pain at that moment, even though I suffered severe injuries, I was again thankful God gave me adrenaline and peace instead of panic. Through the dark times, I knew the only way to get through it would be to rely on my faith and those around me to bring me back into the light of God.

\*

JEWEL ROSE
Jewel was 39 when she and her family
were hit by a drunk driver in 2012

Yes, my faith has been impacted. I never doubted God. I never doubted His love for me. I now get angry when I hear "God allowed this to happen." No, he didn't! This earth is fallen. Bad things happen because bad things happen. God did not want a drunk driver to run my family over. He didn't want the driver to get drunk. Yet, He gave the driver free will. God was there when my world was falling apart. He was there when I could not think. He was there when my son became a person I did not know. He was there when my other son shouldered all the household chores that others couldn't do. He was there when my husband felt alone, and He was there when my father died.

My faith was not shaken, but I did come to the realization that God does not dish out bad things to teach us a lesson. If we learn a lesson from a bad event in our lives, it is because we are faithful to hope, and hope comes from Him!

*

MICHAEL SMITH
Michael's 39-year-old brother Patrick
was killed by an impaired driver in 2007

Yes, my faith was impacted. I didn't understand how a god could possibly let such a good person suffer such a horrible death.

*

LINDSAY WELDON
Lindsay was 21 when she was
hit by a drunk driver in 2012

My faith struggled a bit at first, and became stronger over time. It's the main reason I am where I am today with this whole crash stuff.

*

RACHAEL WILLIAMS
Rachael was 25 when her 30-year-old husband
Matthew was killed by a drunk driver in 2012

My faith in the justice system is the only faith I have lost. There was a reason he was taken. I still attend church regularly and had my children baptized.

*

SHELLY WOODWARD
Shelly was 30 when her 16-month old son was injured in a
drunk driving crash caused by Shelly's former husband in 1996

My faith was impacted at first. I asked God why. Why did he do this? Why did you allow my baby to get injured? But then I reached out and I knew my answer. God could have made my baby an angel that night and he didn't. He could have made things much worse and he didn't. What he did was show me this person needed to go. I honestly don't think anything less traumatic would have made me do that. I learned a very valuable and painful lesson. People have often asked me if I could change the past would I and my answer is no. Every lesson, pain, heartache and joy has made me who I am.

*

# CHAPTER THIRTEEN

# CONFESSING OUR STRUGGLES

*Walking with a friend in the dark is better than walking alone in the light. -HELEN KELLER*

Suicidal thoughts occur for some in the immediate aftermath of tragedy, yet few readily admit it for fear of being judged or condemned. While there would be no rainbow without the rain, have you felt suicidal in the aftermath of the crash?

\*

JESSICA WEYER BENTLEY
Jessica was 5 when her 24-year-old father
Robert was killed by a drunk driver in 1979

I think we all have those thoughts. After Dad was killed, I had them for years as a teenager. I missed my dad so much. I wanted badly to be with him. I was in a very dark place. I thought of it daily but I knew if I just kept going something amazing would happen, and it did. I worked through it by continuing to find ways to help others and through my faith in God.

\*

SHANNON BOOS
Shannon was 20 when her 21-year-old brother
Kevin was killed by a drunk driver in 2015

Before Kevin even died, I was having mental issues. I was battling depression and anxiety. Kevin was one of the few people in my life who actually stood by me through it all. He was by my side through every up and down, and was one of the rare people who actually cared enough to check on me. Had I realized that I was going to lose him just a few months later, I would have thanked him a million times over.

After Kevin was killed, I was swallowed into depression's hole deeper than I had ever been. Getting out of bed was physically painful, and any sort of effort to get back into my normal routine was dreadful to think about. I wanted to die; I wanted to be with my brother more than anything. Wherever he was, I didn't care, I would go. I wanted to be there and protect him and hold him, and he could do the same for me. I made the mistake of telling this to someone, and the person threatened to call the police and have them take me to a hospital. Although I understood why, I was just trying to be honest. Why would I want to be in a world where my brother was gone?

I actually came close to committing suicide one time, although I don't remember it at all. I had been prescribed medication by a psychiatrist to help with anxiety and panic attacks. In reality, I would take one whenever the pain was too much. I wanted to be consumed by sleep so I could drown out the screams in my head and the roar of emptiness in my heart. I would typically take this medication in the afternoon as part of my new routine. I would wake up, lie in bed, take the medication, and sleep until about 7 p.m. Then I would get out of bed, drink a bottle of wine, and pass out again, drunk. It was a vicious cycle, but I didn't care. Nothing mattered anymore, and this was the closest thing I could feel to being dead without actually killing myself.

The only thing that kept me from actually killing myself was to spare my parents and my other brother the pain. I now know firsthand what it was like to lose a sibling so traumatically, so I couldn't put my brother through that. I also saw the gut-wrenching pain that my parents were feeling every single day. The first time in my life that I ever saw my father cry was when we had to pick out a casket for Kevin, and I can still picture it over a year later. I could never willingly put my father or my mother, or anyone else for that matter, through something like that all over again.

One day the pain was substantially worse than usual. I could not sleep or eat. I couldn't even really breathe. I decided to take that magic pill a little earlier than normal. After thirty minutes of not feeling any relief, I decided to take a second pill. And then I blacked out. The next thing I remember is waking up in a hospital and answering questions about my mental history, all the while so exhausted that it was physically painful to speak. Nine hours after I took that second pill, my roommates finally realized something was wrong. My dog was in the same room as me, and was going crazy with panic. My roommates found me unconscious. When I finally came to, I apparently kept saying over and over again, "I want to be with Kevin." I had taken the remaining pills along with Nyquil and a bottle of wine. I later read texts I had sent to my dad in which I kept saying that I was desperate for sleep. I remember nothing.

About a year has passed since this incident, and I am very grateful that I survived. The grief still consumes me at times, but I am fortunate to have found a new love for life and the future. The pain from missing my brother is still immense, but I know Kevin is happy to see a smile on my face, and with eyes on the path in front.

*

TIFFANY COLSON<br>
Tiffany was 30 when she was<br>
hit by a drunk driver in 2011

No, which was surprising, because I have dealt with anxiety

and depression all my life. It has made me a stronger person and made me want to live so that I can be there for my family. I did not die that day, so I want to make sure that my story and others' are heard. Drunk driving is never acceptable.

\*

WENDY DAVIDSON
Wendy was 47 when her 28-year-old son
Chuck was killed by a drunk driver in 2016

I can't say that I felt suicidal, but I did feel that if I also were to have died that day or in the days after, I wouldn't have had to go through the pain that I endured. The only things that kept me beyond those thoughts were my family and my children. The worst part of this whole horrific ordeal, as a mother, is to watch your living children suffer and go through the pain you have spent your life attempting to protect them from. You have absolutely no control. After losing a child, the pain is like dying yourself.

\*

BILL DOWNS
Bill's 21-year-old son Brad, 19-year-old daughter-in-law
Samantha, and 24-year-old family friend Chris
were killed by a drunk/drugged driver in 2007

On December 6, 2012, just five years after the kids' death, my wife told me to get out of the house. The anger that I allowed to control my life had finally reached the point where she could not take it anymore. I was so caught up in the anger and the hatred that I had for God and everybody else, that I couldn't see that my marriage was over. I left and drove to the crash site, and it was then that I decided that life was not worth living. I let go of the steering wheel as I approached the curve where the kids were killed, and that's when God took over. I don't remember driving back home, and to be honest I don't know how I got there.

All I know is God saved me that night, and because of His intervention, saved my marriage.

\*

JULIE DOWNS
Julie's 21-year-old son Brad, 19-year-old daughter-in-law
Samantha, and 24-year-old family friend Chris
were killed by a drunk/drugged driver in 2007

There were many days when I wanted to die, many days I begged God to let me take the place of one of the kids. I curled up in a fetal position, wishing myself dead, crying uncontrollably. But I never wanted to kill myself, so I don't believe that I was having suicidal thoughts, but they were thoughts of desperation. On my worst days, if I had had a gun in my hand, I cannot honestly say I would not have used it. The pain was that unbearable, and I felt such hopelessness. I have never in my life experienced a physical pain as devastating as the emotional pain I felt in my son's death. There were days when I was out of my mind with grief. I couldn't think and I couldn't function. There were days when I thought I was going crazy. I felt that going insane would be easier than fighting it. But with time those feelings of wanting to die turned into feelings of wanting to live and not just to survive. I wanted my life back. I wanted to be happy and I wanted to breathe without crying. In the kids' deaths, I've realized how precious life is.

\*

MICHAEL GERSHE
Michael was 8-weeks-old when his 28-year-old
mother Barbara was killed by a drunk driver in 1970

Have I ever felt suicidal? Many times throughout my life, which is sometimes hard to fathom because I feel that I was kept alive for a purpose. Since I was given this opportunity to live, one might wonder how I could be suicidal  It's called survivor's guilt.

The way I saw it was that my mother had a great life and I was just starting mine. Why keep me alive and not her?

The idea of suicide had nothing to do with having a bad life, it was just feeling such intense internal pain and wanting it to stop. I always wanted to know if my mother was safe. Was she okay? Was she feeling any pain? I wanted to talk to her, to hear her voice, to comfort me as I felt all this pain. I just remember hearing as a kid, "Don't worry, one day you'll meet her again." In my mid-twenties, I wanted that day to come.

One night as I was getting ready for bed I thought about taking a nice dive off my fifteenth floor balcony. I figured I was a swimmer, I could land a nice dive on someone's car. I just wanted to feel at peace from all this pain. That night I had a dream where my mother came to me and said, "Michael, I am fine. Stop worrying about me," and gave me a hug. I woke up face down on the bed with my arms crossed as if I was hugging her. That dream saved my life. My mother once again saved my life.

I remember telling my college roommates, Sean and Big John Kelly, about my thoughts of suicide during a July Fourth barbecue. I was pretty nervous telling them because—let's face it—men don't really open up about this type of stuff to other men, but I knew I had to tell someone. Sean and Big John both lost a parent too, which is one reason the three of us bonded so well in college. When I did tell them, Big John, who was six-foot-four, got upset and proceeded to kick a few panels off the fence in the backyard. He wasn't even kicking all that hard, but down they went with ease. Seeing how they both reacted, I know that no matter how hard it gets, I could never go through with it. Big John died when he was thirty-three, and I saw how his death affected his family and friends. Whenever I have suicidal thoughts, I think back to seeing Big John for the last time, in the coffin, or about being his pallbearer. I couldn't do that to my family or friends. My mother sacrificed her life for me to live, and for me to be a good son who she could be proud of. I could never go through with it—I could never do that to my father, my family or friends.

I have shared these thoughts on stage from time to time and I recall talking to a student once for about an hour after a program. I don't always talk about depression, but on this night I did and she confessed she was having suicidal thoughts that week. It is amazing how many people think about suicide. It's important for them to realize that they aren't alone and that it is not the answer. I work through the pain with humor and by sharing my program.

I have good, bad, and horrible days, and yet as low as I may go, I eventually bounce back to my regular self. It may take time, but I know I have a wonderful support system. I've been blessed with a great sense of humor to help me cope, and I understand my purpose in life. The pain I carry also motivates me to help prevent others from going through it. Besides, I will eventually meet my mother and see my friend Big John again. But not today.

\*

ANNETTE HANKS
Annette was 39 when she and her husband and their
13-month-old granddaughter were hit by a drunk driver in 2013

I have not felt suicidal because of the crash but I have felt like I was going crazy. I thought I must have brain damage from hitting my head, because when I have a flashback I immediately become a sobbing, hysterical mess.

\*

RENE LEDFORD
Rene's 25-year-old son Justin Colt
was killed by a drunk driver in 2015

I have never wanted to harm myself. I sometimes ask God to

give me peace and bring me to Justin Colt, but I wouldn't want to leave my daughters and granddaughter in a life without me, it's already a struggle daily for us without Justin Colt

\*

MELISSA MORIN
Melissa was 30 when she was
hit by a drunk driver in 2013

I remember when I was able to really understand what was going on, which was almost a week later, the doctors explained what was broken and what they needed to do. My mother was with me, it was just us. I remember feeling so devastated that I asked my mother to just roll me down a flight of stairs, and to take care of my son. I'm sure the morphine and drugs came into play, but that's the only time I remember ever having a bad thought to that extent. I have flashbacks of it sometimes, and it makes me cry even typing this. I'm not really one to open up completely. Traumatic events really haunt you.

\*

LINDA PAULSON
Linda was 40 when her husband and their two
young sons were killed by a drunk driver in 2003

To be honest, I think of suicide often. I share my experiences with my counselor. The emotions that are the strongest for me are not being able to have my sons. Missing out on their life. I just want to be with them.

\*

NICOLE RAMOS
Nicole was 32 when she and her two
children were hit by a drunk driver in 2013

When bills started rolling in and insurance was denying payments, this put me in a very dark place. I knew that if I had died, my life insurance would have covered everything, and I wouldn't be struggling with fighting the insurance and answering volatile phone calls from bill collectors. I cried all the time. I felt that our case would have been taken more seriously by investigators if I had died. I never tried to kill myself but played the what-if game quite often. For several months, I felt that it would have been a better outcome if I had died. I did share these dark thoughts with a friend. I told her, "I think it would have been better if I had died in the wreck." This got her heated, and I never brought it up again. I started a private journal and was completely honest in it. I did try to look for the positive because physical therapy was allowing me to do more and more. It wasn't until I actually sat down and told a professional my feelings that I felt validated in everything.

\*

JEWEL ROSE
Jewel was 39 when she and her family
were hit by a drunk driver in 2012

Absolutely. Suicide is very closely related to those who suffer brain injuries. As horrible it seems now, suicide made so much sense to me then. I cannot describe the darkness that filled my mind. I do think I wasn't able to think clearly because of the injury. The workplace antics of my then-boss and then-coworkers certainly added to the thoughts, as well as the antics of the high school principal, who was supposedly dedicated to the protection and wellbeing of every student enrolled in his school.

\*

MICHAEL SMITH
Michael's 39-year-old brother Patrick
was killed by an impaired driver in 2007

Well, no, mainly because now I am the only child remaining to my parents. There have been days when my mind wandered. I don't think I could say it lasted more than five seconds because I was so intensely angry at the man who caused the crash.

*

LINDSAY WELDON<br>Lindsay was 21 when she was<br>hit by a drunk driver in 2012

Not suicidal, per se, but there were times when I was in so much pain, that I wished the crash had killed me.

*

RACHAEL WILLIAMS<br>Rachael was 25 when her 30-year-old husband<br>Matthew was killed by a drunk driver in 2012

I have. I have felt that if it were me who was taken instead of Matthew, things would be better. I have felt like a failure at a lot of things. My depression has taken over and I just wanted to be with my husband again, to be happy, to smile again. Instead, I have two daughters who need me more.

*

SHELLY WOODWARD<br>Shelly was 30 when her 16-month old son was injured in a<br>drunk driving crash caused by Shelly's former husband in 1996

I never felt suicidal. I had severe depression as a teen and this time I had three children who needed a mother. I would never think that way, because of them. I often called friends and family and cried, laughed and talked about it. They have been my rock throughout the years.

*

# CHAPTER FOURTEEN

# HANDLING FAMILY TRANSITIONS

*My family is my strength and my weakness.*
-AISHWARYA RAI BACHCHAN

For many, familial relationships are the cornerstones that help us cope. We speak one another's language and finish one another's sentences. Sometimes, however, tragedies touch us in different ways. What family relationships were impacted most by the crash?

\*

JESSICA WEYER BENTLEY
Jessica was 5 when her 24-year-old father
Robert was killed by a drunk driver in 1979

After the crash, most of my father's family was not in my life. I know my grandmother and grandfather took it especially hard. My grandfather shut himself in his house like a hermit from the 1970s until his death. Most of my family members don't speak about my father, his death, or how it affected them. It happened so long ago. I know my mother and my dad's best friend never visit his grave still to this day, after thirty years, due to the pain and shock of it all. I myself had it really rough. I was traumatized and suffered as a child for years. I still suffer, but as an adult I have a better handle on the grief and pain. It carries on to my children and my husband. My husband has to deal with my nightmares, insomnia, and flashbacks. My children endure never knowing their grandfather. My daughter resembles him. It is hard on them to know that he was taken from them.

*

TIFFANY COLSON
Tiffany was 30 when she was
hit by a drunk driver in 2011

You would think I was the one who was most affected, but it was my husband and our children. It took me a few days to realize what happened. My husband had to endure getting the phone call and then rushing to the hospital without any idea what condition I was in. My kids were young and upset that their momma was hurt. It also hurt others in my family. My husband called my mom, who in turn called other family members. My grandma lived a mile from the hospital and was the first one there, arriving the same time as me but they wouldn't let her see me until my husband arrived. I'm very close to her, so that was upsetting. My mom was upset so my husband sent her in to see me before himself. He brought the kids in once he knew I wasn't paralyzed. The doctors were concerned about that because of my injuries. My kids are now scared of being involved in a car wreck.

*

WENDY DAVIDSON
Wendy was 47 when her 28-year-old son
Chuck was killed by a drunk driver in 2016

Chuck's death has impacted his immediate family the most. He is the oldest brother of my five children. He had shared a home for years with his brother and sister. My second oldest son said to me, "Mom, Chuck was born to be a big brother." He was their confidant, their mediator, their counselor. He offered guidance and a shoulder to cry on if they needed it. These kids would do absolutely anything for each other if they ever needed anything. To say we were close doesn't begin to approach the truth. Chuck's father and I always taught the importance of family, and that nothing ever came before family.

Chuck's brother and sister still live in the same house they shared with their brother. Chuck and his brother were saving to buy a home together. When we opened Chuck's safe, we found almost ten thousand dollars in cash. He had one thousand dollars in his wallet and another twelve hundred dollars in the bank. He was an avid saver and he was saving with a purpose. Sadly, he'll never get to experience buying his first house. Chuck's brother, Chris, received his death benefits and is using that to buy his first home where he can continue to live with his sister. It's bittersweet that Chuck never got to see that purchase to completion, but due to his generosity, his brother Chris is able to. That speaks volumes about the good in Chuck. I'm both proud and sad at the same time.

*

BILL DOWNS
Bill's 21-year-old son Brad, 19-year-old daughter-in-law
Samantha, and 24-year-old family friend Chris
were killed by a drunk/drugged driver in 2007

The crash initially was devastating to both our families. Over time they have moved on with their lives, which is often the case when a death or injury does not personally affect a person's life.

*

JULIE DOWNS
Julie's 21-year-old son Brad, 19-year-old daughter-in-law
Samantha, and 24-year-old family friend Chris
were killed by a drunk/drugged driver in 2007

After the crash comes the impact. Life as we knew it was gone.

There is a void within our family now and no one knows how to bridge the gap. Brad, Sam, and Chris are missing and everyone deals with it differently.

Family gatherings are not the same. We do not celebrate holidays like we use to. No gift exchange at Christmas or fireworks on the Fourth of July.

Brad, Sam and Chris' death happened so fast that no one had time to adjust to the change it caused. It was such a shock. They are talked about in the past tense now, if they are even talked about. It's like they existed in another lifetime. Their death has made everyone look at their own lives and see the many things that are taken for granted. As a family unit, we are broken. We have a deeper understanding now on how quickly things can change and how precious everything is.

*

MICHAEL GERSHE
Michael was 8-weeks-old when his 28-year-old
mother Barbara was killed by a drunk driver in 1970

When you experience a tragedy such as the drunk driving crash that killed my mother or injured me to where no one knew if I was going to live, I don't think anyone is ever the same. My father lost his wife, the mother to his young boys and his soul mate. My aunt lost her younger sister, her parents a daughter. My brother and I lost our mother and it will impact us for the rest of our lives.

I remember when my paternal grandfather passed away in early 1995, and I went to Long Island for his burial. It was the first time I ever visited the cemetery where my mother was laid to rest. I will never forget my father's reaction upon seeing my mother's grave. To see him hurt like that yet still have the strength to be there for his boys is quite amazing. I remember him sitting on a bench a few feet away and just staring at the family plot, lost in his own thoughts. It's an image I will never forget; it inspires me every time I do my program, because that is what I am trying to prevent.

The impact of the drunk driving crash led me down a path to create The Magic of Life program because I feel we all have a purpose, and that this is mine. My brother teaches kids how to swim, so we are both doing something to saves lives. I figured our mother would want us to lead productive lives and help people if we could, and this is the best way we know how. We've seen enough death through drunk driving and kids drowning, and we just said, "Enough." Now we both work to prevent death.

*

ANNETTE HANKS
Annette was 39 when she and her husband and their
13-month-old granddaughter were hit by a drunk driver in 2013

We are all still affected emotionally. We are also all determined to fight DUI driving.

*

RENE LEDFORD
Rene's 25-year-old son Justin Colt
was killed by a drunk driver in 2015

Since Justin was killed, my oldest daughter has lost her faith in God. My younger daughter has gained more faith, as I myself have. My parents do most of the chores Justin did. We try to help but it only makes it more real that he is gone. I've lost all interest in being a wife; my husband is not my kids' biological dad. I cannot get that night out of my head, the thoughts of my son laying all alone in the road, or him hitting the truck and being thrown back. I will never get over him never being here with us again. I am in a mother's grief group and hear that this is normal, which is why a lot of parents divorce after a child dies. My nephew, Colten, and Justin were starting their own business. It took Colten a little longer than planned, but he started their dream business called C & J Pressure Washing. I couldn't be more proud of my nephew.

\*

MELISSA MORIN
Melissa was 30 when she was
hit by a drunk driver in 2013

It has definitely been life changing. We are all in a good place now. This was the family's first major crisis, so to speak. I think my poor mother suffered emotionally as much as I did, but we got through it together. She was my caretaker during recovery.

\*

LINDA PAULSON
Linda was 40 when her husband and their two
young sons were killed by a drunk driver in 2003

It affected my family in so many ways. My oldest son is still messed up by it.

\*

NICOLE RAMOS
Nicole was 32 when she and her two
children were hit by a drunk driver in 2013

My family has been impacted in many ways from the wreck. My son, Elijah, was four when the wreck changed our life forever. He speaks about it frequently and wonders what life would have been like if I could walk better, or not be in pain. He asks about how I used to be and what I could do before. It broke my heart when he drew school pictures of me in a wheelchair or using a cane. He also talks about if we had been in a smaller vehicle, we would have died. He points out compact cars and asks, "What would have happened if we were in that car?" He is fearful of people who are not paying attention, or driving recklessly.

My daughter, Audrey, was thirteen at the time of the wreck and felt guilty because we were out at that time picking her up from a party. She also felt helpless because she saw what I had to endure physically and there was nothing she could do to change it. Now, she is driving and still has some fear of others out on the road and those who drive impaired. My husband was not in the wreck, but definitely suffered from having to take time away from work, and was given a hard time by his administration. The relationship between my husband and I was strained for a while because intimacy was impossible and still is complicated. We have learned to communicate better but we've had a few rough patches because I feel that my pain hinders me from my regular duties and responsibilities. The feelings of anger, rage and frustration have faded away, but sadness and fear still haunt us every now and then.

\*

JEWEL ROSE
Jewel was 39 when she and her family
were hit by a drunk driver in 2012

My sisters wanted to celebrate my fortieth birthday, a family tradition. I did not want to disappoint them. While waiting to board the airplane, I saw that another passenger had brought along his service dog. I desperately wanted one of my own. I will never forget the terror I felt waiting for the tiny commuter plane to arrive. I was so afraid of getting lost in one of the smallest airports in the northwest. I was able to complete this trip with little problem, but I learned that airplane passengers nor my extended family would understand the nuances of my injury. They were supportive, but the next time we got together three years later, they could not understand why I wasn't better. How could I travel to Mexico yet not be able to drive six hours to my mom's? Driving is certainly harder on your body than flying in an airplane. You're expected to rest on a vacation, which is what I did. But when I set boundaries while visiting my family at Christmas, it was very clear that I was being tolerated, and was no longer welcome.

Any issues that exist prior to a brain injury get worse, not better. My fatigue increased, and my inability to participate in games was gone because I could not think fast enough to keep up like I used to. My extended family will never understand, and my immediate family does not understand why it's so hard for me to just be *me*. Why can't I ski and wakeboard like I used to? What about running? None of those things are easy now, because I can't remember how. I struggle to get my body to do what my brain tells it to. Even if my body and brain communicate, I am so tired that I fear I will break another bone. I broke my nose and got another concussion after the accident while just trying to be the old me.

\*

MICHAEL SMITH
Michael's 39-year-old brother Patrick
was killed by an impaired driver in 2007

It began a slow disconnect with my partner of many years. We were not in the best place anyway, and the amount of focus I spent trying to obtain information and force the State of Connecticut to do something about my brother's death drove a wedge between us. My performance at work decreased, and my interaction with other people began to fade, as I was no longer interested in going anywhere or doing anything.

\*

LINDSAY WELDON
Lindsay was 21 when she was
hit by a drunk driver in 2012

My family was impacted financially, at the very least. They lost a car, paid my medical bills, and were there if I needed anything. Mom took time off work to take care of me, and they have been there for me every step of the way.

*

RACHAEL WILLIAMS
Rachael was 25 when her 30-year-old husband
Matthew was killed by a drunk driver in 2012

This has affected my family greatly. Our children will never know what kind of man their dad was. They will never get that chance to go to a daddy-daughter dance or have him walk them down the aisle. For me, it has created a lot of feelings and I have changed. I'm no longer trusting. I have two children who are my primary focus. Matthew's mother is currently in a nursing home with advanced dementia.

*

SHELLY WOODWARD
Shelly was 30 when her 16-month old son was injured in a
drunk driving crash caused by Shelly's former husband in 1996

There is little to no contact with my child's father. His mistakes have made my children smarter, and they do not drink and drive. It has gotten me active in local MADD chapters, and it's been an awakening to people when they hear my story. My youngest is in college to be a veterinarian.

*

Surrender to what is. Let go of what was.
Have faith in what will be.

SONIA RICOTTI

*

# CHAPTER FIFTEEN

# CONFRONTING OUR FEARS

The oldest and strongest emotion of mankind is fear,
and the oldest and strongest kind of fear is fear of
the unknown. -H. P. LOVECRAFT

Fear can cut like a knife and immobilize us like a straitjacket. It whispers to us that our lives will never be the same, and our misfortunes will manifest themselves again. How do we control fear so it doesn't control us?

\*

JESSICA WEYER BENTLEY
Jessica was 5 when her 24-year-old father
Robert was killed by a drunk driver in 1979

I am in constant fear of cars hitting me, to be honest. Whether I walk or drive, I am on constant guard. When something like this happens, many fear the rug being pulled out from underneath again, and losing another loved one. I am never relaxed and am always on high alert. The anxiety and panic can be overwhelming.

My fear was realized when my husband, son, and I were hit by a drunk driver on Labor Day last year 2016. The offender was on drugs and alcohol. We were lucky in that my son and myself were not injured in any way other than psychologically. My husband suffers from some back issues and headaches, and is currently in therapy. The fear is always, always at the forefront of my mind.

\*

SHANNON BOOS
Shannon was 20 when her 21-year-old brother
Kevin was killed by a drunk driver in 2015

I am most afraid of losing someone else. I've lost people before Kevin, but it was never a loss like this. I've lost grandparents who were sick, and distant relatives whom I was never really close to. But a loss like this is something that I can't even compare to anything else.

I remember when two girls from my high school were killed by a drunk driver. It was about two years before Kevin was killed. At the time, I knew one of the girls' brothers, not well, but I knew him. I remember seeing him a few months later and staring at him in disbelief that he was surviving after losing a sibling that traumatically. I couldn't even imagine losing one of my brothers. Two years later, I went through the exact same thing. And now I can imagine it.

Sometimes I get into deep thought about death. I can actually picture myself losing other people, other loved ones. How would I handle it if my dad died? My mom? My other brother? It's not an "I can't imagine" thought anymore. I can imagine. I can feel it deep in my heart and in my soul. I have felt a pain I thought I would never feel, and I never want to feel it again.

I understand that death is inevitable. Everyone dies, it's natural. But the way my brother died was not natural in any sense of the word. I don't want to lose anyone like that ever again that quickly. Here one minute, and gone the next. No time for goodbyes or "I love you." Just gone.

I still jump when my phone rings. I get horrible flashbacks of the phone call saying that my brother had been in a car crash. It isn't so scary when it happens in the middle of the day, or when it's my mom, who calls me just about every day. It *is* scary when it's a person who doesn't call often or at a strange hour. When that happens I immediately think, who died? What happened? Is everyone okay? It ends up being just a regular, ordinary phone call except my heart is beating ten times faster than normal.

I hope that all my loved ones die peacefully many years from now, and that I never go through something like this again. Because this is something I will never recover from.

\*

TIFFANY COLSON
Tiffany was 30 when she was
hit by a drunk driver in 2011

I'm not afraid of much in this world. I like to live that way, but after the wreck I do get nervous driving, especially after dark. I'm afraid that someone is going to run into me for no reason.

\*

WENDY DAVIDSON
Wendy was 47 when her 28-year-old son
Chuck was killed by a drunk driver in 2016

I recently met a man who lost three of his children. When I met him, I felt humbled. My biggest fear is that I will have to live through another one of my children dying. I have become hypervigilant as to their whereabouts, even while being a few hundred miles away. I don't want to go through this again. Having a child die is not the normal process of things. It's not natural. Children are supposed to bury their parents, not the other way around. All clichés have a kernel of truth; now I know why this cliché is true.

*

BILL DOWNS
Bill's 21-year-old son Brad, 19-year-old daughter-in-law
Samantha, and 24-year-old family friend Chris
were killed by a drunk/drugged driver in 2007

I often fear for the safety of our families when I know that not only are there impaired, drugged and distracted drivers on the roads with us daily; but sometimes we wonder if our family members are driving distracted and impaired.

*

JULIE DOWNS
Julie's 21-year-old son Brad, 19-year-old daughter-in-law
Samantha, and 24-year-old family friend Chris
were killed by a drunk/drugged driver in 2007

Fear consumed me as soon as I learned that my kids had been killed. I closed myself up in my house for two years, because I was afraid to face the world and deal with what had happened. It was easier for me to just hide from life. The times I did try to leave the house, I had panic attacks that left me lifeless. I was afraid to live. I didn't know how to continue on with a broken heart.

In facing the death of the kids, it made me realize that I could possibly lose someone else whom I love. Death became real, and if it happened once, it could happen again. If my husband was five minutes late getting home, I would call him to see where he was. If I heard a siren, I would call everyone in my family to make sure it was not them. I kept my handicapped daughter in my sight to make sure she was okay. I was frantic with fear, realizing I had no control over death.

Before the kids were killed I had taken life for granted, but after the crash nothing seemed concrete. Before the crash I had been a people person; I would talk to anyone and everyone. But after the crash, I feared being around people. I avoided conversations for

206

fear that someone would ask how I was doing, how my kids were, or how many kids I had. My mind was in such turmoil that I couldn't keep my thoughts straight or talk without breaking down crying. I felt so vulnerable and lost. I even feared crowds, which included family gatherings. It was hard for me to see everyone laughing and having a good time when I was dying on the inside. I even had a hard time understanding how they could be so happy when my world had come to a standstill. So instead of enduring the pain or putting on a fake smile, I just stayed home.

But the thing I feared most was forgetting my son, forgetting what his voice sounded like, forgetting his laughter, forgetting his smile, forgetting his love. I would sit for hours looking through pictures, memorizing everything about him. I would cry, clinging to all my memories. It seemed like I was torturing myself, but I just wanted to remember everything about him. I never want to forget where his birthmark is or the mole on his forehead or even the bald spot in his eyebrows that seemed to come to a point. I don't want to forget the way he would look at me and say, "Mom, I got it covered." I didn't want to forget that he was double-jointed, afraid of the dark, or that he didn't like mixed vegetables but loved chicken and dumplings. I have twenty-one years of memories, and each one is more important to me than gold. Memories are all I have left, so I don't want them to slip away. My fears have lessened over the years, but will always be part of the new person that is now me.

*

MICHAEL GERSHE
Michael was 8-weeks-old when his 28-year-old
mother Barbara was killed by a drunk driver in 1970

I have some fears that still exist and some that I can control. They may seem silly, but they do impact my life. I sometimes fear not being the son my mother would be proud of, which I know is silly, but I think about it. We all want to please our parents and having this fear, I think motivates me to speak out against drunk driving as much as possible. I know I am not the best son every day. I have a feeling she would be proud of the person I have become but never hearing it from her is the hard part.

Another fear I have is that I am not doing enough to help prevent drunk driving. While I have made this my mission in life, I wonder if I am doing enough. I fear that I won't be able to fulfill my mission for the nonprofit I started to help families who experience drunk driving. Every time I see a news story or hear from someone impacted by drunk driving, it affects me. I fear for those people who have to sort through the hell that is now their lives.

I fear that I am so obsessed with trying to prevent drunk driving that I will continue to sacrifice my personal life at times. There are times where I wish I could just feel "normal" and not have to think about it but I cannot. I have put so much focus and attention into the program, I know my life cannot always be this, but I fear that if I don't do it, no one else will.

I fear that the system will never give families the justice we deserve when it comes to impaired driving. I am afraid the law is not in our favor, and impaired drivers who injure and kill do not face enough punishment. I am afraid that more families will feel this pain, and life is tough enough without this type of experience.

At times I fear driving or biking because there are so many impaired or distracted drivers on their phones. I would love to go out on Halloween or New Year's Eve and really enjoy myself, but those holidays have been ruined by drunk drivers. As much as I love performing comedy, sometimes I fear getting hit one the way home by an audience member who was drinking at the club.

I fear that society will never get that wakeup call about the seriousness of impaired driving. The statement, "Everyone does it," is something I hear way too often and I am afraid that people only take it seriously once they are personally impacted by it. Too many lives are lost, too many people are injured, and that scares me because the statistics that I see are trending in the wrong direction. I am afraid for that next family who will experience being hit by an impaired driver.

*

ANNETTE HANKS
Annette was 39 when she and her husband and their
13-month-old granddaughter were hit by a drunk driver in 2013

I am constantly terrified of something bad happening to my granddaughter. I don't ever want to see her hurt again. And that has morphed into being terrified that something is going to happen to my service dog. He's so amazing and helps me so much, I can't imagine my life without him.

*

RENE LEDFORD
Rene's 25-year-old son Justin Colt
was killed by a drunk driver in 2015

I'm most afraid of losing another child, or my granddaughter, or a family member. Every time the phone rings after 10 p.m., when someone who doesn't call a lot, or when someone goes on a trip, I'm terrified they're not coming back. I've lost my firstborn and so much of myself, I don't want to lose anyone else.

*

MELISSA MORIN
Melissa was 30 when she was
hit by a drunk driver in 2013

I still dislike driving. I even bought a new car hoping that it would give me motivation, but nothing. It has gotten better, so I'm going to hope that with more time it will continue to improve. Since the crash, I am also very conscious and pay attention to other drivers, and have even reported a few drunk drivers!

*

LINDA PAULSON
Linda was 40 when her husband and their two
young sons were killed by a drunk driver in 2003

I am afraid of cars and driving with other people. I fear people leaving me and never coming back.

*

NICOLE RAMOS
Nicole was 32 when she and her two
children were hit by a drunk driver in 2013

When I was in a wheelchair, walker, or cane, I felt very vulnerable to being attacked. I knew that I would be unable to defend myself or my children. I had nightmares that we were being followed home by a man who would force his way into the house, and I could not run or fight back. I also had nightmares about meeting Cody, the drunk driver, through a mutual friend or bumping into him at the grocery store. When I started driving again, I hated being in the lane closest to the yellow line. It reminds me of how unprotected you are from oncoming traffic and how one small infraction by the other driver can change life in an instant. I also had trouble driving at night and seeing oncoming headlights, but that didn't last as long as that yellow line.

I have been cut on and rehabbed so many times, and still feel limited and that I will never be able to do some of the things I love. I fear that my children will only remember me the way I am now, and not the person I was before. I hate meeting new people and having to explain the scars or why I struggle to get around. It comes up all the time. I fear that this will never settle, and I will continue to receive bills and letters from insurance agencies telling me that they are not going to cover my medical care.

*

MICHAEL SMITH
Michael's 39-year-old brother Patrick
was killed by an impaired driver in 2007

After my brother was killed I realized that I wasn't immortal. Believe it or not, I became afraid to fly, especially the takeoff. I would imagine all kinds of terrible things that could happen to the plane. The noises from takeoff freaked me out literally and I had to take pills given to me by a neighbor who is a nurse so I could calm down and not be as uncomfortable. Has it improved? A little, but now I am more cautious than ever.

*

LINDSAY WELDON
Lindsay was 21 when she was
hit by a drunk driver in 2012

My fears have definitely changed over time. At first, I was afraid of the street, afraid of bumping into the drunk guy, afraid to sleep, and afraid to leave the house. Now my fear is that this nightmare happens to more people every day. Nobody takes this crime seriously. I live in a college county, and I constantly hear people joke about drinking and driving. It infuriates me.

*

RACHAEL WILLIAMS
Rachael was 25 when her 30-year-old husband
Matthew was killed by a drunk driver in 2012

Anytime there is something to do with my oldest daughter's school, or music concerts, or Girls Scouts ceremonies, I cry because her dad would have loved them. He would have been so proud. I fear driving at night, even though it can happen at any time of day.

I fear finding love again because he was, and still is, the love of my life.

\*

SHELLY WOODWARD
Shelly was 30 when her 16-month old son was injured in a
drunk driving crash caused by Shelly's former husband in 1996

I really don't have any fears. My ex-husband's wife sent some pretty nasty notes, and he asked me to stop talking about it because it happened so long ago. He has forgotten, but we can't. We do not mention his name when we speak. My mom always said that the guilty speak first. I will not be silent if it saves one person from getting behind the wheel after drinking.

\*

CHAPTER SIXTEEN

# SEEKING COMFORT

*The trick is to be grateful for our good moods and graceful in our low moods. The next time you feel low, for whatever reason, remind yourself that this too shall pass. -RICHARD CARLSON*

Transition sometimes feels as if we have embarked on a foreign journey with no companion, compass, or light. As we fight our way through the storm, what brings the most comfort?

*

JESSICA WEYER BENTLEY
Jessica was 5 when her 24-year-old father
Robert was killed by a drunk driver in 1979

I find writing poetry or reading a good book to be helpful. My husband and I cook together and experiment with recipes, and that bring happiness and soothes those feelings. When things get really bad, I like to walk or get into a pool or hot tub, which I find soothing. I pray a lot for guidance and use prayer as a meditation.

*

SHANNON BOOS
Shannon was 20 when her 21-year-old brother
Kevin was killed by a drunk driver in 2015

The thing that brings me the most comfort is signs from Kevin. I notice them all the time, and in the smallest of things. I don't know if I believe in God, but I do believe Kevin has to be somewhere. An amazing person with a beautiful soul doesn't just disappear. He has to be somewhere. And wherever he is, I know he is trying hard to communicate with me and let me know that he is okay.

I have dreams of Kevin telling me he is okay. I have dreams of him hugging me. I see his face in strangers who look so much like him that it makes me look twice. I see butterflies and birds that fly right in front of my face and snap me out of sad, grieving thoughts.

The first time I visited Kevin's grave by myself, I just sat there. I was crying and talking to him, not sure if he could hear me. I felt like I was wasting my time so between tears I said out loud, "Kevin, if you're here and you can hear me, please, *please*, just give me some sort of sign." A butterfly came. It didn't just flutter by — it flew in circles around my head for about fifteen seconds. I cried, and laughed and smiled, and said "Hi, Kevin!" THAT brings me comfort, along with believing that I can still feel his love and our bond even though I can't see him.

*

TIFFANY COLSON<br>Tiffany was 30 when she was<br>hit by a drunk driver in 2011

After the wreck I watched a lot of television. It helped me to not think about the pain and trauma. I had been through a lot in a short period, and I needed to not think about it. Music helped a lot also. Once I could concentrate, I began knitting again.

*

WENDY DAVIDSON<br>Wendy was 47 when her 28-year-old son<br>Chuck was killed by a drunk driver in 2016

My son absolutely loved music; he played guitar and had three of them. We are a family of music lovers. I play the drums, my husband plays guitar — it's just what we do. In some instances I've found that music helps, but for the most part it's too painful to even hear. The biggest comfort I've gotten thus far is simply being at home, or trying different ways to keep my son's name out there to anyone who will listen.

My home feels safe to me, but beyond those walls there is no comfort, not yet. To me, my son will never be dead as long as I can keep talking about him. I struggle to find new meaning in life and do things solely that keep me from breaking down, things that just make me feel better that day. The next day, maybe a whole new set of challenges and rituals will make me feel better. I just never know.

*

BILL DOWNS
Bill's 21-year-old son Brad, 19-year-old daughter-in-law
Samantha, and 24-year-old family friend Chris
were killed by a drunk/drugged driver in 2007

I drive by the crash site each day and blow the horn three times, which is my way of saying hello to my kids. I find comfort in listening to music my son created on the computer. Though we know the kids are asleep in Jesus, going to the cemetery and spending a little time at the gravesite is comforting.

*

JULIE DOWNS
Julie's 21-year-old son Brad, 19-year-old daughter-in-law
Samantha, and 24-year-old family friend Chris
were killed by a drunk/drugged driver in 2007

When you suffer a sudden loss, there is no time to prepare for the pain that comes, so you seek comfort in many ways. I immediately clung to my son's pillow. He had lain his head on that pillow for the last year of his life. He slept on it the night before he was killed, so I clung to it as a lifeline. I held it tightly and let it absorb my tears. That pillow became a representation of holding my son in my arms. I remember shopping with Brad, picking the pillow out for him. We had just come back from a Disney World vacation, and the hotel we stayed at had goose down pillows. As we were leaving the hotel room for the last time, Brad wanted to sneak the pillow out in his suitcase. He was only teasing, but I told him that as soon as we got home we would shop for goose down pillows, because we had all enjoyed sleeping on them, and that is exactly what we did. I've slept with that pillow for eight years now, and I will never give it up.

I also take comfort in knowing that my son was at his happiest when he took his last breath. He had found his world in Samantha, and was so excited about the life they were going to have together. They had been married only three and a half months. They were so in love, and I'm glad they both had the chance to experience that type of deeply committed love. He always said he wanted the type of marriage and love that his dad and I shared. I do believe he found it with Samantha, and lived it for a very short time.

I was very close to my son. I take comfort in that because I have no regrets in the relationship I had with him. He knew I loved him and I knew he loved me. Not a day went by where he didn't tell me he loved me. Even if he was mad at me, he would come to me before he went to bed to make sure things were okay between us, and to tell me goodnight and that he loved me. The times he was away from home, I would get a phone call at the end of the day from him telling me that he loved me.

And the thing I take the most comfort in is that the last thing we said to each other was "I love you."

\*

MICHAEL GERSHE
Michael was 8-weeks-old when his 28-year-old
mother Barbara was killed by a drunk driver in 1970

Knowing that I almost didn't have a life, I try to be a stop-and-smell-the-roses type of person. Over the years I've found many activities that bring comfort and help me find inner peace when I need it most. I've been coping with being hit by a drunk driver my entire life, so being a kid at heart is always a great comfort. As a kid, I swam, played with Star Wars toys, performed magic, and that all helped. As an adult, I love to read and workout, even though I don't swim anymore, and go see movies for a little escape.

Within the last year or so, hiking around the great parks of northeast Ohio brings me great comfort and peace. It's an amazing escape to hear and see animals in nature. In fact, I get upset when I see people on the trails talking on their phones. I just want to smack the phones out of their hands and say, "Take a look around and embrace this!" I've also gotten into photography and take pictures while I am out hiking, which also soothes raw nerves.

Thank goodness I was blessed with a sense of humor because making people laugh has always brought me happiness. Whether it is in my office, with a friend, or on stage in front of a bunch of strangers, making someone laugh is awesome. I love the creative process of writing a joke, wondering how it will go in front of people, and then performing it. When the audience laughs, it's total euphoria. Of course when they don't, it just makes me work harder to get it to work!

There are two places where I feel the most alive, the first is being on stage and making people laugh. The second place where I feel the most alive is at a KISS concert. Thanks to my brother, I've been a KISS fan since second grade when he introduced me to the band. Whether it's blasting their music or going to a concert, it's total escapism. Heck, I wrote my entire portion of this book listening to KISS! Gene Simmons and Paul Stanley are two of my biggest role models who inspired me to pursue my dreams. When I go to one of their concerts, once those lights go down, whatever is bothering me completely disappears. It's the same feeling I get when the lights go down at a comedy club. It's my job to make people forget their lives outside the club. KISS taught me how to stand up for myself and to enjoy life no matter how hard it gets. While I've never put the makeup on, it's hard to get that smile off my face after a KISS concert.

If any of the aforementioned fails, I'll just go for a pizza and ice cream for comfort!

*

ANNETTE HANKS
Annette was 39 when she and her husband and their
13-month-old granddaughter were hit by a drunk driver in 2013

I think the only thing I remember making me feel better was snuggling and loving on my granddaughter; seeing the miracle of who she was made me happy. Today if I am having a bad day or something reminds me of the crash, I just pick up my phone and call my granddaughter. Her sweet voice makes everything okay.

*

RENE LEDFORD
Rene's 25-year-old son Justin Colt
was killed by a drunk driver in 2015

My daughters, granddaughter and some of my family have been my strong point. We are a very close family and I believe this has brought us closer. Justin Colts absence is felt every second, and my family and I talk about him daily, and have so many memories to share. He will never be forgotten.

\*

MELISSA MORIN
Melissa was 30 when she was
hit by a drunk driver in 2013

Family! And the power of prayer! Those both matter the most. Nothing compares to the ones you love!

\*

LINDA PAULSON
Linda was 40 when her husband and their two
young sons were killed by a drunk driver in 2003

Looking at my kids' pictures and keeping their memory alive have helped me the most.

\*

NICOLE RAMOS
Nicole was 32 when she and her two
children were hit by a drunk driver in 2013

Immediately after the crash I sought comfort in the Ellen Show. She is so optimistic, and I needed that role model in my life. I was in a rough place so Ellen's dancing, spreading cheer, and having a positive message every day really made a difference. I started to think about the positive things about my wreck, and pointing out how it was "perfectly bad timing." If I had swerved to avoid the impact, we would have been hit in the door which probably would have been fatal. If the ten-day-old baby in the other vehicle had still been in his mother's womb, because of her severe injuries it's more than likely he wouldn't have survived. Instead, he was completely unharmed.

I also started reading while lying in a hospital bed for three months. I like to engage my brain in a fictional world and relate to other characters just to take a break from my upside-down world.

Today, I choose to speak about the impact impaired driving has had on my life. I've shared with my students, strangers in the grocery store, church groups, and friends. Using my voice to try to prevent this from happening to someone else is very comforting. I am here for a reason. I lived for a reason. I find comfort in the fact that God has given me another day to advocate for those who also experience this.

\*

MICHAEL SMITH
Michael's 39-year-old brother Patrick
was killed by an impaired driver in 2007

Nothing brings me comfort. The memory is always there. Sure, there are distractions, but comfort? Nothing.

\*

LINDSAY WELDON
Lindsay was 21 when she was
hit by a drunk driver in 2012

I find comfort in crocheting, music, coloring in an adult coloring book with gel pens, hanging out with friends, and lying in bed and binge watching "Friends." I cuddle with my service dogs and find comfort in them. In the initial aftermath, I found comfort in my bed and our family dog.

\*

RACHAEL WILLIAMS
Rachael was 25 when her 30-year-old husband
Matthew was killed by a drunk driver in 2012

We moved after the crash, and changed our way of living. When it's Matthew's birthday, we release balloons and eat cake. We take flowers to his memorial site, which I still find hard to visit. We do the same on Father's Day, but my daughters make their own flowers to place at his memorial site. What brings comfort today? Knowing that my daughters will always know him. We keep his pictures out and speak of him daily. He is missed so very much.

\*

SHELLY WOODWARD
Shelly was 30 when her 16-month old son was injured in a drunk driving crash caused by Shelly's former husband in 1996

My family and my other children brought the most comfort to me after the crash. It is the same circle of friends and family who remain my comfort zones today.

\*

Education is important, but we're to the point where almost everyone knows they shouldn't drink and drive. The people who are still doing it are choosing to do it.

DAVID KELLy

*

# CHAPTER SEVENTEEN

# FINDING FORGIVENESS

Forgiveness is not always easy. At times, it feels more painful than the wound we suffered, to forgive the one who inflicted it. And yet, there is no peace without forgiveness. -MARIANNE WILLIAMSON

According to the Merriam-Webster Dictionary, the definition of forgiveness is to stop feeling anger toward someone who has done something wrong or to give up resentment. It is a voluntary process for which a victim undergoes a change of heart. Is it possible to forgive an impaired driver for getting behind the wheel?

\*

JESSICA WEYER BENTLEY
Jessica was 5 when her 24-year-old father
Robert was killed by a drunk driver in 1979

I work daily to try to forgive the person who killed my father. I have the understanding that people make mistakes and have demons of their own. I lived with an alcoholic stepfather, so I understand that people aren't always aware of the damage they cause. I realize this man is not a monster, but just a man. I pray that one day I can truly forgive him and let it go completely. After thirty years I am still praying for the ability to forgive. When someone just takes an entire human from you, it is quite impossible to forgive them. We are all human and sometimes I do believe there are things that are simply not forgivable. My definition of forgiveness is to come to the complete understanding that the person who did this is sorry, and has learned from the mistake they made. They have changed their life for the better, and though what happened was terrible, this person has shown great regret. I have not seen that here. I may never get an apology. So, forgiveness? I am not sure about that yet.

\*

TIFFANY COLSON
Tiffany was 30 when she was
hit by a drunk driver in 2011

I didn't know the driver who hit me. He was a stranger that I have seen one time in my life. That was at his sentencing. I know that he was punished and hopefully has changed his ways. I like to just live my life not worrying about him.

\*

WENDY DAVIDSON
Wendy was 47 when her 28-year-old son
Chuck was killed by a drunk driver in 2016

Someone mentioned to me the idea of forgiveness and how it healed them. To be honest, the idea of forgiving the individual who took my son's life literally made me sick to my stomach. Some would define me as a tree-hugger. You know the type, the one who wants to save the planet, help others, volunteer, etc. I have never wished or wanted harm done to anyone. To an extent, I still don't, however, I want the drunk driver to suffer as much as my entire family has. Not by death, but by losing his freedom.

There are always consequences to one's actions, either positive or negative, and I want this individual to suffer the consequences. No one will ever know the pain and suffering that comes with the loss of a child unless you go through it yourself, and there is an inherent need during this whole grief process to achieve some sort of justice. I often wonder if I was one of those parents who never got the opportunity for justice (hell, I still may not see justice), what would appease my grief? What about those parents whose child's killer died themselves? Does that count? Are they robbed of their own justice? What about the individual's family, what they must have to go through with their loss and knowing their loved one killed someone? I've been trying to place myself in his family's shoes, but right now I really don't care what they're going through. I don't care if they lose this individual to fifteen years in jail. I just don't care. I've tried not to focus on the justice part of it because I know deep down I'll never be satisfied. So, for now I'm more focused on the notion of trying to heal myself.

\*

BILL DOWNS
Bill's 21-year-old son Brad, 19-year-old daughter-in-law
Samantha, and 24-year-old family friend Chris
were killed by a drunk/drugged driver in 2007

It took me over four years after the kids' death to finally reach a point where I could forgive the drunk driver. Just recently, my wife and I drove out to where she is buried. As we stood there looking over her gravesite, we actually felt sorry for her because it was so poorly kept. Apparently no one had been there in a while. I chose to forgive the driver — not for her, but for myself. Only then would I find peace and move forward.

\*

JULIE DOWNS
Julie's 21-year-old son Brad, 19-year-old daughter-in-law
Samantha, and 24-year-old family friend Chris
were killed by a drunk/drugged driver in 2007

You forgive someone who steps on your toe, lies about you, or slaps you in the face. But how do you forgive the person who killed your child?

For two years after the crash, forgiving the woman who killed my kids was not an option. It was impossible. I have never hated anyone like I hated the drunk driver. She was killed in the crash also, and I was glad. I saw her as the devil himself. Not knowing this person or what she even looked like, I pictured her as a monster or even someone with horns, a pitchfork and a tail. Her choice to drink and drive destroyed my life. It hurt my child, and hurting my child was one thing that as a parent I could not tolerate. You could do whatever you wanted to do to me and I could forgive, but you didn't mess with one of my kids. And that is exactly what she had done.

Brad, Samantha and Chris' lives were just starting. Their future was ahead of them. Brad and Samantha had hopes and dreams of a beautiful life together. Brad was working on a promotion at his job and Samantha had plans to attend college and become a teacher. They wanted to build a home and fill it with babies. Chris had just started a new job with medical and retirement benefits, and felt like his life was finally on track. But then a woman who had no respect for herself or anyone around her selfishly turned her vehicle into a weapon and brutally murdered my kids. How could that act be forgiven?

I knew what the Bible said, *For if you forgive others for their transgressions, your heavenly Father will also forgive you. But if you do not forgive others, then your Father will not forgive your transgressions* (Matthew 6:14, 15). I didn't think that God meant you had to forgive when something this devastating happened to you. He meant that you were to forgive the little things. Besides, I was mad at God so my heart was closed to His word. But I struggled with the thought of forgiving.

The hate and anger were eating me alive. I was becoming a hateful, bitter person. I felt lost, hopeless, and stuck in the mud spinning my tires and not getting anywhere. Each day was the same—full of pain, tears, hate and anger. I was alive, but I wasn't living. Not only had the drunk driver stolen my kids, I was allowing her selfish act to totally destroy me.

As I allowed God into my heart, I realized that the only way things were going to change for me was when I forgave the drunk driver. My mind and heart fought over this. I couldn't forgive her because I felt that if I forgave her, I would be saying that what she did was okay. And I would have to let my son go, and I could never let go of my son. Never!

One day I had a dream that spoke to my heart. I really hadn't dreamed before this. I couldn't sleep at night, so I slept as much as I could during the day because sleep was the only peaceful time for me. In the dream, God was in Heaven holding Brad's arms and I was standing on earth holding Brad's legs. God kept trying to pull Brad up, but I held on tightly as I pulled him back to me. It was like a game of Tug of War.

God said, "Julie, if you are ever going to find peace, you are going to have to give him to me."

I cried, "No, you can't have him," and pulled as hard as I could. The struggle went on for a while, and God's comforting, loving voice kept ringing out until I finally let go of Brad's legs. I gave my precious son to God. I fell to my knees crying, but felt a sense of peace flow through me. I woke up crying, clinging to Brad's pillow, but filled with a sense of peace.

Several things happened over the next couple of weeks that brought me to the realization that if I wanted to live, and I mean really live, I had to release the hurt, bitterness and anger and give it to God. So as hard as it was, I made a choice to forgive the drunk driver. I did not do it for her, I did it for me. I've come to understand that holding on to things that are done against us only hurts us more. Forgiving does not in any way say that what was done is okay, but it does release the control the other person has on you. By holding onto unforgiveness, I became a prisoner of my own bitterness, hate and anger. Releasing those things and forgiving the drunk driver has set me free.

*

MICHAEL GERSHE
Michael was 8-weeks-old when his 28-year-old
mother Barbara was killed by a drunk driver in 1970

Forgiving the drunk driver who killed my mother and almost myself is something I've struggled with throughout my life. There are days when I think I can forgive him, but I just don't think I have it in me. I often read about people who can forgive someone for a horrible crime and I think that is great—for them. But I don't think I have that ability. How do I forgive someone for changing my life in an instant because he drove drunk? He didn't just change my life, but my father's life, my brother's life, and the lives of my mother's family. He ruined so much on the night of September 19, 1970, I'm not ready to forgive him.

By not forgiving him, it doesn't mean I'm always angry or bitter about the crash, just that he took so much from us by his decision to drive that night. I don't know if he had any remorse and since he lied to the police that night and refused to plead guilty for a long time, proves to me that he had very little remorse. I never had the chance to confront him, to look into his eyes to see if he did have any remorse and perhaps that would help with forgiveness.

I can forgive someone for cooking a bad steak or scratching my car (it's a lease), but for killing my mother? I never knew the sound of her voice, the feel of her touch, or her smile. Forgiving him won't bring her back and won't change my life. I don't hate the guy, I let go of that hate a long time ago. But it doesn't mean I forgive him. I doubt I ever will.

*

ANNETTE HANKS
Annette was 39 when she and her husband and their
13-month-old granddaughter were hit by a drunk driver in 2013

It took me a long time and a lot of prayer to be able to forgive our drunk driver. I told him in court that I forgive him and that I would be praying for him. When I heard he was still drinking and driving, being human, I got mad and in doing so discovered I had taken back the forgiveness I gave him. It's been a tug of war with forgiveness and unforgiveness. It's a work in progress! I do know that my forgiving him is only for me, it's not for him. He has to be able to forgive himself and decide to change his ways.

*

RENE LEDFORD
Rene's 25-year-old son Justin Colt
was killed by a drunk driver in 2015

Just a few weeks before he was killed, my son told me that one day I would have to forgive someone for killing him or his sisters. I told him I never would. He responded back saying, "God forgives you every day. How do you expect God to forgive you if you can't forgive someone else?" I live by those words every day.

In my victim statement, I told the young man what my son had said. I then told him, "I forgive you, as I want you to forgive yourself." And with all my heart, I do forgive him. I don't hate him, I hate the choices he made that night. I pray for him every day just as I pray for everyone.

\*

MELISSA MORIN
Melissa was 30 when she was
hit by a drunk driver in 2013

Absolutely not. I'll never forgive him. When I gave my impact statement in court, I actually told him I hated him and would never forgive him. His poor decision altered lives forever and robbed four families. Our lives will forever be changed. I don't ever see myself forgiving him. To be honest, I can't tell you what my definition of forgiveness is. Sometimes I have a hard time accepting the things that I can't change. People's true colors show in times of tragedy. I've found it easier to just let go, too blessed to be stressed or deal with one-sided people.

\*

LINDA PAULSON
Linda was 40 when her husband and their two
young sons were killed by a drunk driver in 2003

I have not forgiven the driver, and I am not sure I ever will. My definition of forgiveness is excusing their bad choice.

\*

NICOLE RAMOS
Nicole was 32 when she and her two
children were hit by a drunk driver in 2013

I have forgiven my impaired driver. Without ever facing him or having justice by the court system, I have turned from anger and vengefulness to forgiveness. I want nothing more than to be able to meet face-to-face and give him insight of what he ran away from that night. I want him to know the physical and emotional pain that has had a ripple effect on my family. I trust that God will work on his heart, and I'll continue to pray that he finds a different lifestyle than drinking and smoking his pain away.

*

LINDSAY WELDON
Lindsay was 21 when she was
hit by a drunk driver in 2012

Yes, I have forgiven the driver, and he actually read it. I never thought I'd forgive him, ever. I knew I needed to, but it took me almost four years.

*

RACHAEL WILLIAMS
Rachael was 25 when her 30-year-old husband
Matthew was killed by a drunk driver in 2012

I will never forgive him. He wasn't sorry for taking my husband. He showed no remorse. At the sentencing, he sat with a smirk and refused to speak or even say sorry. He felt he was not guilty. My definition of forgiveness is one who is sympathetic for the loss of someone, who knows that person was wrong and accepts that they are sorry, and they truly know how it's affecting that person.

*

SHELLY WOODWARD
Shelly was 30 when her 16-month old son was injured in a
drunk driving crash caused by Shelly's former husband in 1996

I am not able to forgive him. I feel like this is something he could stop if he wanted to. I don't buy into the notion that drinking is disease. It is a habit, and he still does it to this day. He has health issues and almost killed his oldest child, which should have been an awakening. I cannot forgive someone who is in denial, and never admits he is wrong or apologizes.

*

Hope. It's the only thing stronger than fear.

ANONYMOUS

\*

# CHAPTER EIGHTEEN

# DISCOVERING HOPE

Be like the birds, sing after every storm.
-BETH MENDE CONNY

Hope is the fuel that propels us forward. It's the promise that tomorrow will be better than today. Each breath we take and each footprint we leave is a measure of hope. But tragedy has a way of redefining hope. What does hope mean to you today?

*

JESSICA WEYER BENTLEY
Jessica was 5 when her 24-year-old father
Robert was killed by a drunk driver in 1979

I remember hope. When I was little, hope was huge to me. I always had it. It was always there and even after Dad was killed I had it. I use hope cautiously now. I tread easily with it. I have noticed as I have gotten older that I have replaced the word *hope* with the word *pray*. I pray you get well. I pray we make it tomorrow. I pray things work out for the best.

I guess hope is just smaller now. I still believe in living on and living big because life ends so quickly but I just don't use that word. Hope seems like a naïve word, juvenile in a sense. I guess maybe I am just cautiously optimistic. Hope is something I cannot afford.

\*

SHANNON BOOS
Shannon was 20 when her 21-year-old brother
Kevin was killed by a drunk driver in 2015

I believe that hope is the feeling you get when you know that no matter how horrible things are now, it will get better. Although life without Kevin is so dark and unbearable at times, I hold on to the hope that I will see him again. Wherever he is, I will be there one day and he will be waiting. He will have that big goofy grin on his face, and will give me the huge hug that I've needed for so long. "Shannonnnnnnnn! I missed you!" And he'll look at me as if it has only been a day or two like we're just meeting up for coffee. I'll collapse into his arms in happiness, unable to stand because of the overwhelming relief. I'm finally with my best friend again.

Hope for me is believing that somewhere out there is a world where Kevin Boos exists with a huge smile and one dimple on his cheek. He is surrounded by mashed potatoes, Pop-Tarts, music, and all our loved ones. He is waiting for me, and I will be there with him. Some day.

\*

TIFFANY COLSON
Tiffany was 30 when she was
hit by a drunk driver in 2011

Hope to me is having a dream. It's what keeps me looking to tomorrow and not letting this hold me back.

\*

WENDY DAVIDSON
Wendy was 47 when her 28-year-old son
Chuck was killed by a drunk driver in 2016

Hope? All my desires that derive around the word hope will never be fulfilled. I hope that I will see my son again. I hope that he will walk through the door and this has all been a terrible mistake. I hope my grief will end soon. I hope that I will feel whole again. I hope no one will ever die at the hands of a drunk driver ever again. Hope has no meaning to me today other than I hope I make it through the day. I hope I have a better day tomorrow than I did today. I hope my children will come through this horrific event without a lifetime of scars or torment. Hope is a very foreign word to me now.

*

BILL DOWNS
Bill's 21-year-old son Brad, 19-year-old daughter-in-law
Samantha, and 24-year-old family friend Chris
were killed by a drunk/drugged driver in 2007

For me, you can't have hope without having faith. I know I can focus on helping others through the hard times of losing someone or being injured by an impaired, drugged or distracted driver. Each time I see a smile because something I said or did has helped them in some way, my hope is renewed.

*

JULIE DOWNS
Julie's 21-year-old son Brad, 19-year-old daughter-in-law
Samantha, and 24-year-old family friend Chris
were killed by a drunk/drugged driver in 2007

I believe that hope can be found through hopelessness. When something tragic happens like it did the night Brad, Samantha and Chris were killed, despair and hopelessness can consume you. You can either make the choice to stay there or you can fight your way out of that hopelessness and find hope.

My hope is in God's promise that one day He will wipe every tear from my eyes and there will be no more death or mourning, crying or pain. But until that day I will do my best to be a voice for those who no longer have a voice because of an impaired driver. I will tell my kids' story in hopes that it will save another mother or family from knowing the pain and heartache that could have been prevented by a better choice to not drink and drive.

So, in defining hope I would have to say that hope is Jesus Christ. For the Lord himself will descend from heaven with a cry of command, with the voice of an archangel and with the sound of a trumpet. The dead in Christ will rise first and those who are alive, who remain, will be caught up together in the clouds to meet the Lord in the air, and then we will be reunited with our loved ones who have passed before us. So, *my hope* is in seeing my son again, touching him, holding him, and never ever having to say goodbye.

*

MICHAEL GERSHE
Michael was 8-weeks-old when his 28-year-old
mother Barbara was killed by a drunk driver in 1970

This is a tough question to answer. Throughout my life and the fact I was given a chance to share my story with so many, I think I provide hope with each presentation. I wake up every day with a new sense of hope in regards to our society realizing the danger of impaired driving. I feel like Bill Murray in the movie Groundhog's Day because when I wake up, I think, "Today is the day! Today is the day when society finally understands and I won't read or hear another story about an innocent person killed or injured by a drunk driver." And as much as that hope fades, I have to remain positive, otherwise I can't do my job on that stage.

I believe that by presenting The Magic of Life to any audience, whether it's high school students or DUI offenders, that I can make a difference in their lives. I see a change with the offenders during the program and it's amazing to be part of that process. I hope they leave that courtroom ready to lead a better life and that gives me hope that the message is being heard. Even when I feel hopeless and depressed at times, knowing that someone heard my story and it resonates with them gives me hope for a better tomorrow.

I was kept alive, whether by the doctors or by the grace of God for a purpose. Having the opportunity to share my story takes the tragedy and allows me to make something positive from it. My purpose is to stand up for my mother, my family and for others impacted by impaired driving and I just hope I do right by them every time. If someone has hope, then they can achieve whatever they want in life.

*

ANNETTE HANKS
Annette was 39 when she and her husband and their
13-month-old granddaughter were hit by a drunk driver in 2013

Two years ago, maybe even one, I couldn't speak about the crash without crying my eyes out. Now I speak at a DUI victim impact panel, and half the time I don't cry. Looking back, I never had hope that things would get better, but today I can see that it has gotten a lot better. That is hope to me.

*

RENE LEDFORD
Rene's 25-year-old son Justin Colt
was killed by a drunk driver in 2015

Hope used to mean something different before my son was killed. My hope now is that I choose the right path and fulfill my purpose here on earth, and that it will lead me to be reunited with my son in heaven.

*

MELISSA MORIN
Melissa was 30 when she was
hit by a drunk driver in 2013

My definition of hope: hope is knowing you can weather any storm, and seeing the light at the end of the tunnel.

*

LINDA PAULSON
Linda was 40 when her husband and their two
young sons were killed by a drunk driver in 2003

Hope to me means that, with everything I have been through, I can survive anything that comes my way.

*

NICOLE RAMOS
Nicole was 32 when she and her two
children were hit by a drunk driver in 2013

My definition of hope is having a dream for your future outcome. I hope that I will be given a direction with the new me. I will not be able to contribute to society, friends and family the way I did before. I will have to find my way and create new paths toward a life God can be proud of. I hope that I fulfill my family's needs and push forward even though we have been down a rough road.

*

MICHAEL SMITH
Michael's 39-year-old brother Patrick
was killed by an impaired driver in 2007

This is going to sound terrible, but I am waiting for an impaired diabetic to cause an accident involving someone famous or important. It is the only way I can see the public and especially state officials realizing that this is a very dangerous and largely ignored public problem. There needs to be legislation to watch over people who are at risk of getting behind the wheel with low blood sugar, and to take away the license of those who have a track record of causing accidents in this manner.

The man who killed my brother never even received a traffic ticket for running a red light. His license was suspended at my urging however through his doctor, the State of Connecticut allowed him to reinstate it three months later. Nothing happened to this man. My family, however, was forever changed, and my brother suffered a horrible death. He wasn't killed instantly; eyewitnesses at the scene said he was breathing and moaning for several minutes afterward.

*

LINDSAY WELDON
Lindsay was 21 when she was
hit by a drunk driver in 2012

Hope is a way to bring a positive to a negative situation. I hope for a full recovery, I hope the pain will go away, and I hope for the future.

*

RACHAEL WILLIAMS
Rachael was 25 when her 30-year-old husband
Matthew was killed by a drunk driver in 2012

My definition of hope is a feeling of trusting someone, feeling that something will happen and that it follows through. Today, hope means that I can get another day of happiness, that I can hope my children know what kind of person their dad was.

\*

SHELLY WOODWARD

Shelly was 30 when her 16-month old son was injured in a
drunk driving crash caused by Shelly's former husband in 1996

My hope is that someday my son will accept that his father is out of his life. It took me a long time to stop allowing the negativity in my life from certain family members. Once I did, my life was a positive one. I told my son, this will always be your dad, but how you want to accept him is your choice. I know he loves his dad, that can't be helped. I just wish he could at least have had a father figure.

\*

# CHAPTER NINETEEN

# MAKING PEACE WITH OUR JOURNEY

Be soft. Do not let the world make you hard. Do not let the pain make you hate. Do not let bitterness steal your sweetness. -KURT VONNEGUT

Every journey is as unique as one's fingerprint, for we experience different beliefs, desires, and needs. Though we may not see anyone else on the path, we are never truly alone for more people walk behind, beside, and in front of us. In this chapter lie the answers to the final question: What would you like the world to know about your journey?

*

JESSICA WEYER BENTLEY
Jessica was 5 when her 24-year-old father
Robert was killed by a drunk driver in 1979

No matter what was thrown at me, I made it through. I survived a hundred percent of the heartache thrust upon me. This journey has taught me a lot about perception and pain. It has taught me that no matter the struggle I experience I have lived through worse. This tragedy has made me strong for my husband and children, and I find peace in that. I will not buckle or give in any more. I will not be a victim. I will have my nightmares, shake them off, get up and move forward. My journey started out dark and bleak, but it will end in light and peace. I believe that, and strive toward it. Just because something terrible happens doesn't mean you have to give in to it. I will finish this life doing everything I can to have wonderful experiences and positivity. I will experience the life my dad was not able to; I will do that for him, and carry him with me.

My journey is just starting. One day when I leave this world, my dad will meet me and that journey will begin. For me, it is a never-ending quest for love and peace. And I will have it, no matter what it takes.

*

SHANNON BOOS
Shannon was 20 when her 21-year-old brother
Kevin was killed by a drunk driver in 2015

I would like the world to know that losing Kevin is something that has affected me permanently, and has changed who I am as a person forever. This isn't a breakup with a boyfriend, this isn't a broken bone; half of my soul was taken from me.

Whether a stranger, a friend, an acquaintance or a family member is reading this, you should know that my grief isn't going to go away. I will never get over it, I will never "move on."

I wrote a poem to express how my grief has impacted me, and how it affects me every day. I wrote it for myself because writing has always been an outlet for me. I wrote it for others who are on this horrible journey with me, so they will know they're not alone. But mostly I wrote it for those who tell me to move on, who think that this is something I could possibly get over. I wrote it for those who are fortunate to have never felt pain like this, hoping that just maybe they can try to understand.

## GRIEF
### BY SHANNON BOOS

It may sound like a calm, somber feeling to you.
It sounds soft.
It sounds like smooth waves that strike you
above your stomach when days are hard.

But grief is relentless and unforgiving.
It is still waters, suddenly erupting into towering waves,
knocking you to the ground, leaving your lungs full of water,
not sure which way is up as you gasp for any sign of air.

Grief is not sleeping soundly in the night, waking up with a few tears.
It is being torn to consciousness as pain decides to dig
its claws into your chest, daring you to try to breathe.

Grief is not a cloud that hangs over your head.
It is shackles tied to your ankles, your arms, your neck, your heart,
confining you to the pain when all you want to do is live free again.

Grief is not being surrounded by love and
those you rely on holding you up.
It is turning around two weeks after he's gone,
screaming into an empty room because
there's no one there but yourself.

Grief is not a nightmare or two at night.
It is waking up with a pounding heart,
thankful that this was all just a dream.
And then you realize that it wasn't just a dream.

This is real.
This is your new life.
And you have to live with it. Every. Single. Day.
Forever.

\*

TIFFANY COLSON
Tiffany was 30 when she was
hit by a drunk driver in 2011

I want people to know that you are stronger than you think you are. Some days just waking up is an accomplishment, and that's okay. I had to learn this. The person who hit me was only a small part of my journey, and I will not let him control the rest of my life. I have two wonderful kids and an amazing husband who love me. This could have turned out a lot different. So please, do not drink and drive. It is not worth the risk.

\*

WENDY DAVIDSON
Wendy was 47 when her 28-year-old son
Chuck was killed by a drunk driver in 2016

So far my journey has been very short. I'm still traveling, so to speak, and have much road to cover before I find my new normal, as people keep telling me. I will learn. I've gotten some really great advice from people through these two months, and one piece of advice in particular: I will survive this. I will get through this and I will live and honor my son and his legacy until the day I die.

I've learned that taking care of myself is priority, and that I have to take each day as it comes. I always taught my children that there is a positive in everything we do. I'm trying to follow my own advice and keep an open mind to whatever positive may come from this. I just haven't found it yet, and I may never.

*

BILL DOWNS
Bill's 21-year-old son Brad, 19-year-old daughter-in-law
Samantha, and 24-year-old family friend Chris
were killed by a drunk/drugged driver in 2007

My journey down this road of grief is not unlike that of others who have lost or been injured by an impaired, drugged or distracted driver. Each day is a challenge and as long as I stay focused on the path ahead, life will continue. I have seen many doors open since I gave my life to God. God has blessed my wife and me with a nonprofit called AVIDD-Advocates for Victims of Impaired/Distracted Driving. AVIDD's main purpose is to support victims of this horrific crime. Each time I support a victim I become their voice; just as I am the voice of my three kids. God has taken a tragedy and is changing lives through my wife and I. That is, in itself, a great honor.

*

JULIE DOWNS
Julie's 21-year-old son Brad, 19-year-old daughter-in-law
Samantha, and 24-year-old family friend Chris
were killed by a drunk/drugged driver in 2007

Life can change in a blink of an eye. As I held Brad in my arms for the first time, I never dreamed that I would one day have to face his death. The pains of birthing him were nothing compared to the pain of burying him. He did not have to die. But someone made the bad choice to drink and then drive. If she would have called a cab or had a designated driver or had even chosen not to drink at all, Brad along with Samantha and Chris would still be alive.

Each year, over ten thousand people are killed at the hands of an impaired driver. That's one person every fifty-one minutes. Two hundred and ninety thousand people are injured a year. Impaired driving is an epidemic that's out of control. I can't help but wonder if it will ever end. What will it take to get people to understand that alcohol, drugs and driving do not mix! I stood next to Bill looking into Brad and Samantha's grave. Bill took a handful of dirt and dropped it on their coffins and promised them that we would be their voice. We promised to never give up the fight against drunk driving. And we have kept that promise through the nonprofit organization we founded in memory of Brad, Samantha and Chris called AVIDD which stands for Advocates for Victims of Impaired/Distracted Driving. We take every opportunity that we can to tell the kid's story in hopes of saving lives. We speak to DUI offenders about making better choices and to not ever drink and drive again. We go to health fairs, law enforcement events including sobriety checkpoints and even to church festivals sharing information about the dangers of impaired/distracted driving. Our main mission is reaching out to others who have been impacted by impaired/distracted driving. We support the victims of this one hundred percent preventable crime. AVIDD has four online Facebook support groups.

Loss of loved one:
Facebook.com/groups/AVID4DUIvictims

Survived with injury:
Facebook.com/groups/AVID4DUIsurvivors

Distracted driving:
Facebook.com/groups/AVID.Distracted

BUI:
Facebook.com/groups/AVIDDimpairedboatingvictims

We provide a safe haven where victims can come together and share their thoughts and feelings. We are a group of victims helping other victims. If you are a victim of a drunk, drugged, or distracted crash, or crash from someone boating under the influence, please look us up. You do not have to do this alone. There are others who understand and care. Together we can make a difference.

Drunk, drugged, distracted driving STOPS with me! Will it STOP with you?

*

MICHAEL GERSHE
Michael was 8-weeks-old when his 28-year-old
mother Barbara was killed by a drunk driver in 1970

I was eight weeks old when a drunk driver decided to put me on this journey. I believe that we all have powerful stories to share, and the fact that so many shared theirs in this book is amazing. Despite everything we have gone through, we are standing before you not as victims but as survivors. I have my good, bad and ugly days, but through it all I stand tall because although a drunk driver killed my mother, he will not take my soul.

On September 19, 1970, a mother saved her son just like any parent would do for their baby. My mother sacrificed her life so I could live, allowing me to carry on her legacy of making a difference. She was a schoolteacher and made a difference with those kids. This journey is never easy, but then again, making a difference in life never is, right?

It's ironic that I called my program The Magic of Life when I first started back in 1994. I called it that because I was performing magic tricks, which I no longer do, but the name really evolved into something pretty powerful. Nearly every bone in my body was broken, my skull was fractured, there had to be some magic in my survival! No matter how often I get frustrated by the justice system or reading the statistics of people getting DUIs, I try to find the magic in my life and that really helps me survive. We all have that magic we can use on our own journey. If I stop presenting, then the drunk driver wins and I'm way too competitive for that to happen.

How many more people have to die or be injured from impaired driving? When is it finally enough in this country? It's amazing how socially acceptable drunk driving is and when two out of three people will be impacted in their lifetime, it's time to change that perspective. Drunk driving is not a mistake nor is it an accident. A mistake does not cost someone their life. A mistake did not kill my mother, a drunk driver did.

I am honored and grateful every time I am able to present my program which has become a major part of my journey. I am just one mother's son trying to make the world a better place, a safer place so others don't have to go through what I have gone through. This is my life, but it doesn't have to be yours. I don't want you to know what my life is like because you have another journey to live.

Every day I wake up, I want to make my mother proud of what I do. Until the day I meet her again, my journey continues by sharing my story. Because I'm a survivor.

*

ANNETTE HANKS
Annette was 39 when she and her husband and their
13-month-old granddaughter were hit by a drunk driver in 2013

I want people to know that it doesn't mean you're weak if you need help after a trauma. If you need a support system of people who understand, that's totally okay! Seek help, talk to friends, find a victim advocate in your area, just don't be alone in your misery. I promise things will get easier.

*

RENE LEDFORD
Rene's 25-year-old son Justin Colt
was killed by a drunk driver in 2015

Since my son was killed, life is a daily struggle. The okay days are just that, not like they used to be. The bad days are more frequent and take my breath away. The harsh words from others and uncompassionate feelings can drop you to your knees, and you feel like you're getting stomped on over and over. But in reality, it's their *not* knowing that saves them from the torment of emptiness that engulfs you. Some people either don't care or don't have a filter, the attention-wanters, the liars, the ones who think it's all about them when actually it's all about *my* son who is no longer with me. Avoiding these people was my solution, and I still do.

The longing to hear his voice, see his smile, hold him, and to hear "I love you, Momma," one more time is slowly killing me. I've aged double since that night. I not only lost him, but I lost a big part of me too. I'm not going to just snap out of it. My life has changed and I'm trying to make the best of this new life. I know in time it will get somewhat easier, an "easier" that only parents who have lost a child can know. I will never get over losing him. He will always be my son, and I will always be his mom. Until my last breath, I will make sure Justin Colt will always be remembered. There is always going to be someone who will hurt you just because, or the ones who don't know or don't really care. But it's their *not* knowing that makes me forgive. Not forget, but *forgive*.

*

MELISSA MORIN
Melissa was 30 when she was
hit by a drunk driver in 2013

My journey definitely hasn't been easy. From being in the hospital literally broken in pieces, to wanting to give up, to being determined. Quietly crying in the middle of the night. It took me a long time to accept things. Here we are, almost three years later, and I'm still adapting. In any situation, know that there is light at the end of every tunnel, and never give up. Family and faith can get you through anything. I also refused to let anyone tell me "I can't."

*

LINDA PAULSON<br>Linda was 40 when her husband and their two<br>young sons were killed by a drunk driver in 2003

This has been a journey that I never thought I would have to take. This journey has had a lot of twists and turns. Having a strong faith in God has really helped me.

*

NICOLE RAMOS<br>Nicole was 32 when she and her two<br>children were hit by a drunk driver in 2013

I would like the world to know that I am still the same person on the inside, even though my outward appearance has changed. I am not defined by my limitations. I do not want to be pitied or given the easy way out. I want to be able to share, be emotional, and have a tough day every now and then. I need help finding new passions but not being excluded from my old passions merely because I am not who I was. Even though I have finished many surgeries and rounds of physical therapy, that doesn't mean I have completely recovered.

I am still learning how to live this new life I was dealt. Every now and then I struggle and juggle thoughts of how my life could have been if the wreck never happened, if I would have opted for amputation, or if the wreck would have been fatal. I try my hardest to focus on what's in front of me and not behind me, but that is easier said than done. I want those who are thinking the same thoughts and have the same fears to know that life is worth living. I do not take my day-to-day life for granted. Take one step at a time, write down your thoughts, positive or negative. Share your story: it is free therapy, and could change someone's life!

*

MICHAEL SMITH
Michael's 39-year-old brother Patrick
was killed by an impaired driver in 2007

You will never be the same. You will adapt, learn to cope, and move forward. But you will never be the same, and you shouldn't expect to. If you are lucky, as I was, you will change a little, into a more mature version of yourself that looks to the future but remembers the past.

*

LINDSAY WELDON
Lindsay was 21 when she was
hit by a drunk driver in 2012

I want everyone to know that my journey has not been an easy one, but positive things came out of it. I found something to be passionate about, and a story that is completely my own. The crash comes first, then the impact. If anyone is on a similar journey and needs support or wants to talk, I've included an email address where you can reach me. Hang in there.

*

RACHAEL WILLIAMS
Rachael was 25 when her 30-year-old husband
Matthew was killed by a drunk driver in 2012

That it was a hard one. You can be so happy one day, and the next everything is broken and you're left alone. I want you to know

251

that it can happen to anyone, all it takes is one person to be in the wrong. Drinking may not affect you, but your actions while drinking is what can shatter the lives of so many others. Please stay off the road and drink responsibly. You can never pick up the broken pieces of a child. They will forever feel that hurt.

*

SHELLY WOODWARD
Shelly was 30 when her 16-month old son was injured in a drunk driving crash caused by Shelly's former husband in 1996

That there is light at the end of the tunnel. I lost everything I had, including my pride. Material things can be replaced, my child cannot. My pride has mended and I am fine. My life has improved without my son's father in our lives. I have moved on. It has made me stronger and a better person. To get in front of a group of a thousand military men and women and talk about my story and have them come up and hug me, means the world to me. I feel God wanted me down this path for a reason. He knew I wanted to help others. I just never knew in what way that would occur. Now I do.

*

# CHAPTER TWENTY

# FINDING THE SUNRISE

One night in my grief journey, I had a terrifying dream where I was running frantically to catch the setting sun. Chasing from behind was nightfall, an ominous pitch-black monster coming straight for me, threatening to swallow me whole. I ran as fast as my legs could go toward the sun but my attempt was futile: it descended below the horizon, out of my reach.

Oh, the looming nightfall was terrifying! But I had no choice — if I ever wanted to see the sun again, I had to stop running toward a sunset I couldn't catch. Instead, I had to turn around and walk directly into the pitch-black abyss of grief. Just as there would be no rainbow without the rain, the sun rises only on the other side of night. The dream's message was clear: it was futile to avoid my grief; I had to allow it to swallow me whole. Then — and only then — would I find my way through it and out the other side.

I remember reading in a bereavement book that if we don't allow ourselves to experience the full scope of the journey, it will come back to bite us. I couldn't fathom how it could get any worse, but I knew I didn't want to test that theory. So I gave in and allowed the grief to swallow me whole. I allowed myself to wail on my daughter's bedroom floor. I penned my deep emotions regardless of who might read it. I created a national radio show to openly and candidly discuss our journeys with anyone who wanted to call in. And I allowed myself to sink to the bottom of the fiery pits of hell. Doing so lit a fire under me, so to speak, to find a way out.

Today I'm often asked how I manage my grief so well. Some assume that because I have found peace and joy, I'm simply avoiding my grief. Others believe that because I work in the bereavement field, I'm wallowing in self-pity. Well, which is it?

Neither. I miss my child with every breath I take. Just like you, I will always have my moments and triggers: the painful holidays, birthdays, death anniversaries, a song or smell that evokes an unexpected memory. But I have also found purpose, beauty and joy again. It takes hard work and determination to overcome profound grief, and it also takes the ability to let go and succumb to the journey. Do not be afraid of the tears, sorrow, and heartbreak; they are a natural reaction and imperative to our healing.

As you walk your own path, avail yourself of whatever bereavement tools ease your discomfort, for each one was created by someone who walked in your shoes and understands the heartache. While there are many wonderful resources available, what brings comfort to one person might irritate the next. Bereavement tools are not one-size-fits-all, so if one tool doesn't work, find another.

Lastly, grief is not something we get *over*, like a mountain. Rather, it is something we get *through*, like the rapids of Niagara Falls. Without the kayak and paddle. And plenty of falls. But it's also survivable. And if others have survived this wretched journey, why not me? And why not you?

Following are the baby steps I took to put hell in my rearview mirror. At first they took great effort and lots of patience. But like any dedicated routine, it got easier over time, and the reward of finding balance in my life was worth every step.

## 1. VALIDATE YOUR EMOTIONS

The first step is to validate your emotions. When we talk about our deep heartbreak, we aren't ruminating in our sorrow or feeling sorry for ourselves. By discussing it, we are processing it. If we aren't allowed to process it, then it becomes silent grief. Silent grief is deadly grief.

Find a friend who will patiently listen while you discuss your loss for fifteen minutes every day. Set the timer, and ask him or her not to say anything during those fifteen minutes. Explain that it is important for you to just ramble without interruption, guidance, or judgment. You need not have the same listener each time, but practice this step every day.

## 2. COMPASSIONATE THOUGHTS

Find yourself a quiet spot. It can be your favorite chair, in your car, in your office, or even in your garden. Then clear your head and for five minutes think nothing but compassionate thoughts about yourself. Not your spouse, not your children, not your coworkers, but yourself. Having trouble? Fill in the blanks below, and then give yourself permission to really validate those positive qualities. Do this every day.

I have a _____

Example: good heart, gentle soul, witty personality

I make a _____

Example: good lasagna, potato salad, scrapbook, quilt

I'm a good_____

Example: friend, gardener, knitter, painter, poem writer

People would say I'm _____

Example: funny, kind, smart, gentle, generous, humble, creative

## 3. TENDER LOVING CARE

While grieving, it is important to consider yourself as being in the intensive care unit of Grief United Hospital, and treat yourself accordingly. How would nurses treat you if you were their patient in the ICU? They would be compassionate, gentle, and allow for plenty of rest. That is exactly how you should treat yourself. Also, soothing your physical self with tender loving care is an attentive way to honor your emotional pain. This doesn't mean you have to book an expensive massage. If wearing fuzzy blue socks offers a smidgen of comfort, then wear them unabashedly. If whipped cream on your cocoa offers a morsel of pleasure, then indulge unapologetically.

Treating our five senses to anything that offers a perception of delight might not erase the emotional heartache, but it will offer a reminder that not all pleasure is lost. List five ways you can offer yourself tender loving care, and then incorporate <u>at least three</u> into your day, every day. With practice, the awareness of delight eventually becomes effortless, and is an important step toward regaining joy.

SUGGESTIONS:

- Shower or bathe with a lovely scented soap
- Soak in a warm tub with Epsom salts or a splash of bath oil
- Wear a pair of extra soft socks
- Light a fragrant candle
- Listen to relaxing music
- Apply a rich lotion to your skin before bed
- Indulge in a few bites of your favorite treat
- Enjoy a mug of your favorite soothing herbal tea
- Add whipped cream to a steaming mug of cocoa
- _____

## 4. SEE THE BEAUTY

Listening to the birds every morning was something I had loved since childhood. But when Aly died, I found myself deaf and blind to the beauty around me. One morning while lying in bed, I vaguely noticed the birds chirping outside my bedroom window. My heart sank as I realized that they had been there all along, but I was now deaf to their beautiful singsong. Panic set in as I concluded I would never again enjoy life's beauty. Briefly entertaining thoughts of suicide, I quickly ruled it out. I couldn't dump further pain on my family. But in order to survive the heartbreak, I had to find a way to allow beauty back into my life. From that point forward, I forced myself to listen and *really hear* the birds. With persistent practice, it became easier and then eventually effortless to appreciate the singsongs.

Profound grief can appear to rob our world of all beauty. Yet the truth is, despite our suffering, beauty continues to surround us. The birds continue to sing, flowers continue to bloom, the surf continues to ebb and flow. Reconnecting to our surroundings helps us to reintegrate back into our environment.

Begin by acknowledging one small pleasantry each day. Perhaps your ears register the sound of singing birds. Or you catch the faint scent of warm cookies as you walk past a bakery. Or notice the sun's illumination of a nearby red rosebush. Give yourself permission to notice one pleasantry, and allow it to *really* register.

SUGGESTIONS:

- Listen to the birds sing (hearing)
- Observe pretty cloud formations or blooming flowers (sight)
- Visit a nearby park and listen to the children (hearing)
- Light a fragrant candle or bake cookies (scent, taste)
- See the beauty in the sunset (sight)
- Attend a local recital, concert, play, or comedy act (hearing)
- Wear luxury socks, a soft scarf or sweater (touch)

## 5. PROTECT YOUR HEALTH

After our daughter's accident I soon found myself fighting an assortment of viruses including head colds, stomach flu, sore throats and more, compounding my already frazzled emotions. Studies show that profound grief throws our body into "flight or fight" syndrome for months and months, which is very hard on our physical bodies. Thus, it becomes critical to guard our physical health. Incorporating a few changes into our daily routine feels hard at first, but soon gets easy. Plus, a stronger physical health helps to strengthen our coping skills.

Below are a few suggestions to add to your daily routine to help your physical self withstand the emotional upheaval.

- Practice good sleep hygiene
- Drink plenty of water
- Take a short walk outside every day
- Resist simple carbohydrates
- Keep a light calendar, guard your time carefully, and don't allow others to dictate and overflow your schedule

## 6. FIND AN OUTLET

For a long time in the grief journey, everything is painful. In the early days, just getting out of bed and taking a shower can be exhausting. Housecleaning, grocery shopping, and routine errands often take a back seat or disappear altogether. As painful as it is, it's very important to find an outlet that gets you out of bed each day. Finding something to distract you from the pain, occupy your mind, and soothe your senses can be tricky, but possible. Performing a repetitive action can calm your mood, and even result in a new craft or gifts to give.

Beginning a new outlet may feel exhausting at first, but remember that the first step is always the hardest. And you don't have to do it forever, just focus on it for the time being.

SUGGESTIONS:

- Learn to mold clay or make soap
- Learn how to bead, knit, crochet, or quilt
- Volunteer at a local shelter
- Learn a new sport such as golf or kayaking
- Create a memorial garden in a forgotten part of the yard
- Join Pinterest
- Doodle, draw, or learn to paint
- Join a book club or scrapbooking group

## 7. LAUGH EVERY DAY

One laugh can scatter a hundred griefs. True story. It's also important to understand that the heart can hold joy at the same time it holds sorrow. Laughter really helps to fill the joyful side and balance out the sorrow.

Grief is hell on earth. It truly is. But when walking through hell, your only option is to keep going. Eventually the hell ends, the dark night fades to dawn, and the sun begins to rise once again.

Just keep going and you too will find the sunrise.

*Lynda Cheldelin Fell*

CREATOR, GRIEF DIARIES
www.LyndaFell.com
www.GriefDiaries.com

One smile can change a day.
One hug can change a life.
One hope can change a destiny.

LYNDA CHELDELIN FELL

*

HIT BY IMPAIRED DRIVER

# MEET THE WRITERS

*

JESSICA WEYER BENTLEY
Jessica was 5 when her 24-year-old father
Robert was killed by a drunk driver in 1979

Jessica Weyer Bentley was born in Kenton, Ohio, but spent most of her childhood growing up in the hills of eastern Kentucky. After getting married over twenty years ago, her family relocated back to Hardin County, Ohio, where she currently resides. Jessica received her medical administration degree at Rhodes State College and is currently working as a healthcare documentation specialist at The Orthopaedic Institute Of Ohio in Lima.

She is a member of a local MADD Action Team that supports law enforcement at OVI checkpoints, and many weekends delivers snacks and refreshments to law enforcement to support them in memory of her father. Jessica also volunteers as a speaker at victim impact panels and schools to educate others about the dangers of drinking and driving. In her spare time she writes poetry and has begun to pen her first book, *Crimson Sunshine*. Though she has many achievements, Jessica considers her greatest accomplishment is that of wife to her high school sweetheart, Larry, and mother to her two children, Laura and Joseph.

*

SHANNON BOOS

Shannon was 20 when her 21-year-old brother
Kevin was killed by a drunk driver in 2015

Shannon Boos was born and raised in south Florida. Being the youngest of three and the only girl, she was always described as one of the boys. Now twenty-one, Shannon is studying to become a certified veterinary technician to pursue her passion for animals, and currently works at an animal hospital as a member of the kennel staff.

\*

TIFFANY COLSON
Tiffany was 30 when she was
hit by a drunk driver in 2011

Tiffany Colson was born in Oklahoma, and returned to Texas when she was two days old. She is a married mother of two kids, a boy and a girl. She works as a receptionist. On her days off she enjoys hiking, knitting, and reading when she gets the time. She lives on two acres in the country with her husband, kids, and their schnauzer dog.

\*

WENDY DAVIDSON
Wendy was 47 when her 28-year-old son
Chuck was killed by a drunk driver in 2016

Wendy Davidson was born in Camp Lejeune, North Carolina. She is a network analyst for a major telecommunications company in northern Virginia. She owns an alpaca farm with her husband Jay in the Shenandoah River Valley. She is the mother of five adult children ranging in age from nineteen to twenty-eight. Wendy is a lover of music and enjoys playing the drums along with her husband who plays guitar. In her spare time, she makes every effort to ensure her son's name is never forgotten.

\*

BILL DOWNS
Bill's 21-year-old son Brad, 19-year-old daughter-in-law
Samantha, and 24-year-old family friend Chris
were killed by a drunk/drugged driver in 2007
aviddvoiceofthevictims.weebly.com

Bill Downs was born and raised in southern Mississippi, where he met and married his wife Julie, in 1982. God blessed them with two children, Cynthia and Brad. Bill is twice retired, first from the Air National Guard in 2006 and then from the Gulfport City School District in 2015. His wife Julie is self-employed, and also cares for their handicapped daughter, Cynthia. In 2007 when their son Brad, his wife, Samantha, and Chris, a young man they loved as a son, were killed by a drunk driver. After the kids' death, Bill and Julie's focus turned to advocating and supporting victims of impaired driving. Bill is president and cofounder of AVIDD, (Advocates for Victims of Impaired/Distracted Driving), a nonprofit organization. Bill is also an administrator of four online support groups for victims, and hosts an educational class called AVIDD Voices, where victims share stories with offenders who are court-ordered to attend. Bill is an award-winning author of *Grief Diaries: Loss by Impaired Driving* and *Grief Diaries: Shattered*, with his wife Julie and renowned author and publisher, Lynda Cheldelin Fell.

\*
JULIE DOWNS
Julie's 21-year-old son Brad, 19-year-old daughter-in-law
Samantha, and 24-year-old family friend Chris
were killed by a drunk/drugged driver in 2007
Advocates for Victims of Impaired/Distracted Driving
aviddvoiceofthevictims.weebly.com
avid4duivictims@cableone.net

Julie Downs was born and raised in Gulfport, Mississippi. She graduated from high school in 1978 and completed two years of college before she married her soulmate, Bill Downs, in 1982. She is a housewife and mother of two. Her oldest daughter Cynthia is mentally challenged and still lives at home. Her second born son Brad is asleep in Jesus. After her son's death in 2007 at the hands of a drunk driver, Julie joined and volunteered with MADD until 2014 when she and her husband founded AVIDD-Advocates for Victims of Impaired/Distracted Driving. She devotes her time to operating four online Facebook support groups where she lends a listening ear and makes graphics for members to help bring awareness to the devastation of impaired driving. Julie is an award-winning author of *Grief Diaries: Loss by Impaired Driving* and *Grief Diaries: Shattered.*

\*

MICHAEL GERSHE
Michael was 8-weeks-old when his 28-year-old
mother Barbara was killed by a drunk driver in 1970
info@themagicoflife.org | www.themagicoflife.org

Michael Gershe was born in Suffern, New York, and moved to Miami, Florida, in 1975, where he lived until he left for college. Despite breaking nearly every bone in his body in a drunk driving crash when he was an infant, he earned a swimming scholarship to Ashland University in Ohio, where he earned a degree in communications. He then earned a Master's degree in higher education administration from the University of Akron. While in graduate school, he created The Magic of Life program which combines stand-up comedy with his story for an inspirational non-doom-and-gloom alcohol awareness and impaired driving prevention program. He has been speaking for over twenty years at schools, colleges, military bases and in court. He is also the senior advisor for the College of Applied Engineering at Kent State University. In April 2015, he founded The Magic of Life, Inc., (www.themagicoflife.org) a nonprofit organization that will assist in his mission in preventing impaired driving and help those impacted by it. Michael is a fan of the Miami Hurricanes, Miami Dolphins and a member of the KISS Army.

*

ANNETTE HANKS
Annette was 39 when she and her husband and their
13-month-old granddaughter were hit by a drunk driver in 2013

Annette Hanks grew up in Ephrata, Washington. After marrying her high school sweetheart Wyatt, they moved to Moses Lake where they raised two daughters, Marque and Ashleigh. Wyatt worked as a diesel mechanic and a field mechanic in the agriculture industry. Annette enjoyed being a stay-at-home mom. The Hanks family is very active in their church.

\*
RENE LEDFORD
Rene's 25-year-old son Justin Colt
was killed by a drunk driver in 2015

Rene Ledford was born in Stanton, Texas, in 1971. She grew up in Midland, Texas. She attended Greemwoog High School and studied criminal justice at Midland College. In 1990, she became a mom at the age of eighteen to Justin Colt in Fort Worth, Texas. In 1991, her first daughter, Ariel Nicole, was born and in 1993 Brooke Aaron came along. In 2014, she was blessed with her first grandchild, Kyleigh Nicole.

Rene married her best friend and soulmate, Jesse Estes, in 2011. She and Jesse live in the trailer that Justin Colt gave them in 2012. All his memories are around her house and her parents' ten acres where she and her three kids grew up. She has since joined Stop DWI in Midland, which serves all of west Texas, hoping to save lives one step at a time.

\*
MELISSA MORIN
Melissa was 30 when she was
hit by a drunk driver in 2013

Melissa Morin was born in Chicago, Illinois in 1982. As a kid her family moved around a lot because her dad worked construction. They eventually ended up back in Chicago. She grew up as a normal kid, but every family has their struggles. She dropped out of high school at sixteen but eventually earned her diploma. By eighteen she had moved in with her friend Jill, and they lived together as roommates for several years. She eventually ended up working for her aunt's towing company for ten years. Melissa now works as a contractor for a railroad. She is engaged to an amazing man who is her rock and the father of her handsome three-year-old son.

\*

## LINDA PAULSON
Linda was 40 when her husband and their two
young sons were killed by a drunk driver in 2003

Linda Paulson was born in Englewood, New Jersey, and moved to Illinois. She was mostly a stay-at-home mom, though she did work as a nursing assistant for a time.

*

NICOLE RAMOS
Nicole was 32 when she and her two
children were hit by a drunk driver in 2013

Nicole Ramos was born in Riverside, California, and moved to Texas for college. She earned her B.S. in Child and Family Studies from the University of Texas of the Permian Basin. Nicole coached softball at junior college, high school, and at the competitive level. Her time in the classroom and on the field brought her joy for many years. She also taught four-year-old children at church every Sunday. Her job, volunteering, and coaching came to a standstill one brisk October night when someone chose to drink and drive. She has undergone over nine surgeries and several rounds of physical therapy to try to put her life back together. Her family has been her biggest support system through many difficult times. MADD and AVIDD have been able to relate to the emotional baggage, chronic pain, and day-to-day struggle that comes with being a victim of drunk driving. Nicole is married to Tommy Ramos and has two children, Audrey and Elijah, and three stepchildren, Thomas, Breanna and Sarah.

\*

AMANDA RIDDELL
Amanda was 26 when she and her three
children were hit by a drunk driver in 2003

Amanda Riddell (nee: Dickson) was born the youngest of five children in a small town in the Rocky Mountains of Cranbrook, British Columbia, Canada. Her father worked at Cominco mines in Kimberley, British Columbia, where he and his wife raised their family. Amanda often had a smile on her face while interacting with others and was always helping—right down to giving away her own clothing to those in need as a young child. In her teen years she worked as a volunteer at the local hospital and graduated from the local high school. As a young mother she persevered in her schooling to become an R.N.

\*

JEWEL ROSE
Jewel was 39 when she and her family
were hit by a drunk driver in 2012

Jewel Rose was born and raised in a small town in Washington state. She was an athlete and a college graduate, and earned her teaching certificate while working full time as a paraprofessional in Idaho. She has been married for twenty years, and is raising two very active sons in northern Idaho.

\*

MICHAEL SMITH
Michael's 39-year-old brother Patrick
was killed by an impaired driver in 2007

Michael Smith was born in northern Connecticut, and has lived in Atlanta, Miami Beach, and San Diego. He attended the University of Connecticut and several trade schools, and has worked in real estate and in custom built furniture. In 2014, he moved back to the east coast to be near family.

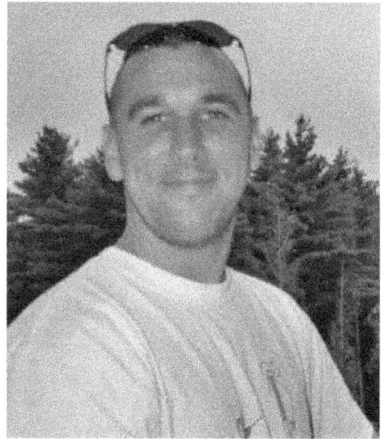

\*

## REBECCA TIMMONS
### Rebecca was 46 when she was
### hit by a drunk driver in 2015

Rebecca Timmons was born and raised in Stuart, Florida. She moved to Michigan when she was seven years old and moved back to Florida at age thirty. She is a mother of three adult children, two sons and one daughter. Rebecca was hired by the Martin County Sheriff's Office in 2001, and has continued to work there for fifteen years as a 911 dispatcher.

\*

LINDSAY WELDON
Lindsay was 21 when she was
hit by a drunk driver in 2012

Lindsay Weldon was born in Fresno, California, and moved to Morro Bay when she was five years old. She attended a local high school where she met two of her best friends, sung and traveled to London with the school choir, and graduated in 2009. From there, she briefly attended a community college where she learned American sign language. She went on and worked a few jobs until she returned to school to become a massage practitioner. Through one of her best friends, she met the love of her life and married him in May 2015. Lindsay hopes to continue learning American sign language and go on to be an interpreter one day.

\*

RACHAEL WILLIAMS
Rachael was 25 when her 30-year-old husband
Matthew was killed by a drunk driver in 2012

Rachael Williams was born in Georgia and raised in Michigan. She is a twenty-nine-year-old widow with two daughters who are four and seven. She recently graduated with her bachelor's degree in long term health administration. She currently isn't working and is spending more time with her children.

\*

SHELLY WOODWARD

Shelly was 30 when her 16-month old son was injured in a
drunk driving crash caused by Shelly's former husband in 1996

Shelly Woodward was born and raised in a small community in Ohio. She has worked in healthcare for over forty years and has written articles for MADD and been a victim advocate speaker since 1999. Shelly is Gigi to three wonderful grandchildren and one deaf rescue boxer dog. Shelly now lives in South Carolina and continues to write for *Divorced Moms* and speak to tell her story.

Shared joy is doubled joy;
shared sorrow is half a sorrow.

SWEDISH PROVERB

\*

# THANK YOU

I am deeply indebted to the writers of *Grief Diaries: Hit by Impaired Driver*. It requires tremendous courage for each writer to revisit such tender memories. The dedication to seeing this book project through is a legacy they can be proud of. I'm also humbled to partner with coauthors Julie Downs and Michael Gershe, two lovely souls I greatly admire for their compassion toward others, and dedication to plowing the field and planting the seeds of hope.

I very much appreciate author Annah Elizabeth's assistance in framing the start of each chapter. I'm also grateful to our Grief Diaries village and the very lovely souls I consider dear friends, collaborative partners, mentors, and muses. I treasure each and every one of you! Finally, it goes without saying how much I love my husband Jamie, our children, and our wonderfully supportive family and friends for being there through laughter and tears.

Helen Keller once said, "Walking with a friend in the dark is better than walking alone in the light." By sharing our struggles, we learn that we aren't truly alone as we travel our journey, for there are others ahead of us, behind us, and right beside us. That is what Grief Diaries is all about.

*Lynda Cheldelin Fell*

She who heals herself
heals others.

LYNDA CHELDELIN FELL

\*

LYNDA CHELDELIN FELL

# MY STORY

When I was a kid, I wanted to be a brain surgeon. But life has a way of throwing us curve balls that force us down a different path. Sometimes those paths are most welcome, like mothering four wonderful children. My least favorite path? Losing a child. That path is a long and torturous one, and took me straight through the belly of hell.

My story began one night in 2007 when I had a vivid dream. My daughter Aly and I were passengers in a car that missed a curve in the road and sailed into a lake. The driver and I escaped the sinking car, but Aly did not. My beloved daughter was gone. The only evidence left behind was a book floating in the water where she disappeared.

Two years later, on August 5, 2009, that horrible nightmare became my reality when Aly died in a car accident. Returning home from a swim meet, the car carrying Aly was T-boned by a father coming home from work. My beautiful fifteen-year-old daughter took the brunt of the impact and died instantly. She was the only fatality.

Life couldn't get any worse, right? Wrong. Hell wasn't done with me yet. My dear sweet hubby buried his grief in the sand. He escaped into 80-hour work weeks, more wine, more food, and less talking. His blood pressure shot up, his cholesterol went off the chart, and the perfect storm arrived on June 4, 2012. My husband suddenly began drooling and couldn't speak. At age 46, my soulmate was having a major stroke.

My dear hubby lived but couldn't speak, read, or write, and his right side was paralyzed. He needed assistance just to sit up in bed. He needed full-time care. Still reeling from the loss of our daughter, I found myself again thrust into a fog of grief so thick, I couldn't see through the storm. Adrenaline and autopilot resumed their familiar place at the helm.

But I needed reassurance that the sun was on the other side of hell. As I fought my way through the storm, I discovered that helping others was a powerful way to heal my own heart. I began reaching out to individuals who were adrift and in need of a life raft. And a warm hug.

In 2013, I formed AlyBlue Media to house my mission. Comforting people who spoke my language and listening to their stories, my mission took on a life of its own and came in many forms: a radio show, film, webinars, and writing. I also hosted a national convention to bring the brokenhearted together. I had many wonderful speakers but the one who excited me most was a woman who had faced seven losses in a few short years: Martin Luther King's youngest daughter. I didn't bring Dr. Bernice King to the convention to tell us about her famous father—we already knew that story. I wanted to know how she survived.

Over the course of that weekend, I was deeply moved by complete strangers swapping stories about hardship. Touched to the core, I set out to capture them into a book series aptly named

Grief Diaries. Over a hundred people in six countries shared stories in the first 8 titles published in December 2015. Now home to more than 600 writers spanning the globe, Grief Diaries has 24 titles in print. More titles are on their way, and I've just launched our second series called Real Life Diaries.

Where am I today? Once a bereaved mother, always a bereaved mother. My heart is a bit like a broken teacup that has been glued back together. All the pieces are there, but they might not fit as seamlessly as they once did. Some days the glue is strong and unyielding. Other days that glue is wet, and threatens to spring a leak. Nonetheless, that teacup still holds water. Well, mostly coffee. Strong coffee.

Life can throw a really mean curveball that blindsides even the strongest. It's important to hold out hope that the sun can be found at the end of the path. But until you find it, it's comforting to know you aren't alone. And that is what my mission all about.

For the record, I have found the sun. Some days I marvel at its beauty. Other days it hides behind clouds. But I now know those days don't last forever. And my umbrella is much stronger than it used to be.

Helen Keller once said, "Walking with a friend in the dark is better than walking alone in the light." If you too are looking for the sun, visit our village for a hug and stay for the friendship. That's why we're here—to offer you a seat in our life raft until the storm passes, and the sun begins to shine once again. I'll even let you borrow my umbrella.

*Lynda Cheldelin Fell*

## ABOUT LYNDA CHELDELIN FELL

Considered a pioneer in the field of inspirational hope in the aftermath of hardship and loss, Lynda Cheldelin Fell has a passion for storytelling and producing groundbreaking projects that create a legacy of help, healing, and hope.

She is the creator of the 5-star book series *Grief Diaries* and *Real Life Diaries*, and CEO of AlyBlue Media. Her repertoire of interviews include Dr. Martin Luther King's daughter, Trayvon Martin's mother, sisters of the late Nicole Brown Simpson, Pastor Todd Burpo of Heaven Is For Real, CNN commentator Dr. Ken Druck, and other societal newsmakers on finding healing and hope in the aftermath of life's harshest challenges.

Lynda's own story began in 2007, when she had an alarming dream about her young teenage daughter, Aly. In the dream, Aly was a backseat passenger in a car that veered off the road and sailed into a lake. Aly sank with the car, leaving behind an open book floating face down on the water. Two years later, Lynda's dream became reality when her daughter was killed as a backseat passenger in a car accident while coming home from a swim meet. Overcome with grief, Lynda's forty-six-year-old husband suffered a major stroke that left him with severe disabilities, changing the family dynamics once again.

The following year, Lynda was invited to share her remarkable story about finding hope after loss, and she accepted. That cathartic experience inspired her to create groundbreaking projects spanning national events, radio, film and books to help others who share the same journey feel less alone. Now considered one of the foremost grief educators and healing facilitators in the United States, Lynda is dedicated to helping ordinary people share their own stories of survival and hope in the aftermath of loss.

lynda@lyndafell.com | www.lyndafell.com

# ALYBLUE MEDIA TITLES

Grief Diaries: Hit by Impaired Driver
Grief Diaries: Surviving Loss of a Spouse
Grief Diaries: Surviving Loss of a Child
Grief Diaries: Surviving Loss of a Sibling
Grief Diaries: Surviving Loss of a Parent
Grief Diaries: Surviving Loss of an Infant
Grief Diaries: Surviving Loss of a Loved One
Grief Diaries: Surviving Loss by Suicide
Grief Diaries: Surviving Loss of Health
Grief Diaries: How to Help the Newly Bereaved
Grief Diaries: Loss by Impaired Driving
Grief Diaries: Loss by Homicide
Grief Diaries: Loss of a Pregnancy
Grief Diaries: Hello from Heaven
Grief Diaries: Grieving for the Living
Grief Diaries: Shattered
Grief Diaries: Project Cold Case
Grief Diaries: Poetry & Prose and More
Grief Diaries: Through the Eyes of Men
Grief Diaries: Will We Survive?
Real Life Diaries: Living with a Brain Injury
Real Life Diaries: Through the Eyes of DID
Real Life Diaries: Through the Eyes of an Eating Disorder
Grammy Visits From Heaven
Grandpa Visits From Heaven
Faith, Grief & Pass the Chocolate Pudding
Heaven Talks to Children
Color My Soul Whole
Grief Reiki


FORTHCOMING TITLES (PARTIAL LIST):
Real Life Diaries: Living with Rheumatic Disease
Real Life Diaries: Living with Endometriosis
Real Life Diaries: Living with Mental Illness
Real Life Diaries: Living with PTSD
Real Life Diaries: Through the Eyes of Child Sex Abuse
Real Life Diaries: Raising a Disabled Child
Real Life Diaries: Life After Rape
Grief Diaries: Through the Eyes of a Funeral Director
Grief Diaries: You're Newly Bereaved, Now What?

Humanity's legacy of stories and storytelling
is the most precious we have.

DORIS LESSING

\*

To share your story, visit
www.griefdiaries.com
www.RealLifeDiaries.com

PUBLISHED BY ALYBLUE MEDIA
*Inside every human is a story worth sharing.*
www.AlyBlueMedia.com

AlyBlue
MEDIA

www.ingramcontent.com/pod-product-compliance
Lightning Source LLC
Chambersburg PA
CBHW031141020426
42333CB00013B/474